Warriors of th...
Native American Regalia & Crafts

By
M.S. Tucker and Joe W. Rosenthal
Illustrated by David W. Rickman

Crow-Style Warshirt. The artistry of the Regalia of Plains Warriors is epitomized by this reproduction of a Crow Warshirt (ca. 1900). The use of contrasting colors and the panoply of ermine hide drops are faithful representations of the original art. A full set of regalia featuring this Warshirt can be seen on Page 53.

This photograph, taken in 1875, shows a group of Sioux visiting Washington, DC on a diplomatic mission. On occasions such as this Sioux men would wear warshirts and warbonnets, an indication of high status. In this photograph we also see that most of these important men were wearing commercial shirts and vests, demonstrating that such clothing was considered appropriate for important occasions.

Published by Crazy Crow Trading Post

P.O. Box 847 • Pottsboro, TX 75076

(903) 786-2287 • www.crazycrow.com

Illustrated by David W. Rickman

Layout Design by Dennis Graham

ISBN 1-929572-24-7

DEDICATION

To Win Fairchild and Hans Duddenhaus. They showed us the way.
To Cindy Tucker and Barbara Rosenthal, our wives. Their patience,
encouragement, and love made this book possible.

ACKNOWLEDGEMENTS

During the many years that we spent studying, researching and making American Plains Indian Outfits we
have received knowledge and encouragement from numerous sources and friends.

We would like to acknowledge all of them and hope that we miss none here.
In our youth both of us read books and articles by Ben Hunt, Bernard S. Mason, Julian Salomon,
and Norman Feder. Their writing about Native American material culture was educational and, more importantly, inspirational. Four more authors were especially important due to their contributions to
our knowledge of ethnography: Carrie Lyford, William Orchard, Alice Fletcher, and Francis La Flesche.
Special thanks are due to these legends in the field.

There have been so many friends that have educated and inspired us over the years.
It would be impossible to overstate their contributions to our knowledge and enjoyment of the field.
It is our pleasure to celebrate the names of James O. Steiner, Chottie Alderson, Bentley M. Stone,
John Stephen Smith, Tyrone H. Stewart, Sylvester Warrior, Abe Conklin, Ida Mae Conklin,
Lamont Brown, Dr. Robert Arriss, Richard E. Troy and Andy Bisaccia.

We also want to thank Adam Lovell, Edward Boone, Jim Ross, Dave Bailey, Marshall Ellis, Clyde Ellis,
David Dean, Bill Holm, Sandy Rhoades, and Jerry Smith for all we have learned from them
and for their friendship.

Very special thanks are due to two gentlemen who graciously allowed us to use many items that they
so skillfully made. We gratefully acknowledge the generosity of our friends, Sam Ornelas and
the late Charlie Johnson.

TABLE OF CONTENTS

Dedication & Acknowledgements 3
Forward 6
Introduction: "The Look" 8
Map of the Plains 10

Chapter 1 "HEADING IN THE RIGHT DIRECTION" 11
How to do Research 12
Where to Find Materials 14
Progression and Craftsmanship 17

Chapter 2 "THE OUTFITS" 18

Central Plains 20

Northern Plains/Plateau 38

Southern Plains 54

Chapter 3 "HOW TO MAKE IT—APRONS AND LEGGINGS" 67

Breech Clout or Aprons? 67

How to Get Started 68

Making a Set of Aprons 69

Apron Progression 71

Making a Set of Leggings 72

Cutting Leather Lacing 73

Central and Southern Plains Cloth Leggings 74

Northern Plains/Plateau Panel Leggings 76

Northern Plains/Plateau Blanket Leggings 78

Chapter 4 "HOW TO MAKE IT—HEADDRESSES" 79

The Coup Feather 79

Clusters and Drops 81

Rigs 82

Headbands 83

Making a Looped Feather 84

Constructing a Rig and Attaching a Looped Feather 85

Single Feather Vertical Rig 86

Single Feather Horizontal Rig 87

Double Feather Vertical Rig 87

Counterbalances 88

Wearing the Roach 89

Roach Spreaders 90

Roach Feathers 92

Attaching the Roach to the Head 94

Roach Placement 95

The Authors 96

Photo Credits 96

FORWARD

There was a time when brave men on buffalo ponies ruled the Great Plains.
There was a time when beads and buckskin, feathers and fur, tradecloth and tomahawks celebrated daring and deeds. It was a long time ago, but the memories linger still and the visions remain a part of our American heritage: the Era of the American Indian Warriors of the Plains.

We still see evocative images of those times in vintage photographs, paintings, and drawings. And we see the shadows of those times in modern day powwows and wardances. This book has been created for craftsmen, young and old, who wish to learn about making the clothing of those great American Indian Warriors of the Plains.

But why do these images so capture our imagination?
The answers are complex, but at least a portion lies in the wonderful craftsmanship that blended the traditional pre-contact materials with those materials that became items of trade in the post-contact era. Thus, the splendid eagle feather warbonnets were well matched with breechclouts and leggings made of tradecloth. Thus, the traditional designs used in porcupine quillwork were skillfully adapted for use in beadwork by the wonderful artists of that era. Thus, the traditional and the modern were juxtaposed with such artistry that more than a century later we still admire the articles they adorned; and there is every reason to believe that they will be admired long, long into the future.

"Charles M. Russell's painting entitled "Running Buffalo", ca. 1918"

"Amos Bad Heart Bull's ledger art drawing of Grass Dancers, ca. 1900"

What are the sources of these images that continue to be such an evocative part of our American heritage? Of course, the paintings of Catlin, Bodmer, Remington, and Russell have stood the test of time; the photographs of Rinehart, O'Neill, Ellsworth, and Kaesebier continue to inspire. And, perhaps most importantly, the vintage ledger art of the American Plains Indians themselves is a powerful source of inspirational images that cannot be surpassed.

What we have learned from these vintage images is that the outfits that we describe in this book were used for dance, for warfare, and for formal or ceremonial occasions.

This book is intended to be neither an anthropological exposition nor an academic treatise. Rather, it is designed to teach aspiring craftsmen how to assemble, from available components, an authentic-looking outfit. Thus, we have avoided the formal language and format of a scholarly work. However, it is not specifically a craft manual. For that task, there are numerous books and articles available that will teach beginners and more advanced craftsmen specific methods and materials for constructing the various outfit components. Nonetheless, we believe there is sufficient information in this book to allow someone with limited experience and skills to get started.

Finally, it should be noted that many, if not all, of the skills used to create the outfits shown in this book can be used to make the kinds of outfits used in contemporary powwow clothing. And the educational process of learning about the history of the complete outfits and their individual components will serve the interests of both the craftsmen who re-create the outfits and those who wear them.

"F.A. Rinehart's photograph of a Southern Cheyenne warrior, Wolf Robe, wearing his Peace Medal, ca. 1898"

This is our rendition of the famous F.A. Rinehart photograph of Goes to War and Hollow Horn Bear. The outfits have been made using materials currently available and are reasonably representative of their vintage counterparts.

INTRODUCTION

"The Look"

The main body of this book consists of photographs and descriptions of outfits and their components for Plains and Plateau tribes. We know that each tribe, no matter where or when, has a style all its own. However, to make this book more general we have divided the Plains into three areas: Central, Northern/Plateau, and Southern; this selection was made based on the similarity of costume of the tribes in each area, respectively. We think the outfits illustrated in each section will serve a craftsman well in terms of authentic appearance. We refer to this appearance of authenticity as "The Look" because it is our intent to illustrate outfits that can be created using either authentic or substitute materials while still retaining The Look of the originals. In addition, we needed to define a period in time upon which to focus. In general, the outfits described here will date from about 1870 through 1930. As one progressed from the early part of this period to the later, outfits became more elaborate. In creating an outfit, it is important to be time-consistent, and to pay attention to era-related details. We have endeavored to do so in the examples shown.

The beginning and intermediate outfits are somewhat generic with regard to tribe. Thus, as one progresses from an intermediate to an advanced outfit, a specific tribe will need to be selected in order to retain both The Look and the authenticity that an advanced outfit merits.

For many, getting started seems a daunting task since there is so much to learn and many of the skills and techniques needed are no longer part of our daily lives. For each area we will show the reader how to get started by illustrating beginning outfits that are, at once, simple and authentic-looking. They are simple because we use only readily available materials and techniques that do not require extensive handicraft skills. They are authentic-looking because they retain the The Look of the original.

Along with beginning and intermediate outfits, we have included many advanced outfits so the beginning craftsman can have a vision of what is possible. We have also designed the components of each outfit in a manner that will allow them to be used for all three categories. That is, a well-made set of beginning leggings could be used, as is, with an intermediate outfit or an advanced outfit. Further, if they are well made, they could be enhanced with beadwork, eliminating the need to start from scratch. We call this approach progression and it is covered in Chapter One.

Two Sioux men, Goes to War and Hollow Horn Bear, epitomize "The Look" of the Warriors of the Plains. Whilst the warbonnets, breastplates, and beadwork bespeak the artistry, their stern visage, along with the rifle, remind us that these men were warriors. Rinehart photo, ca. 1898

Northern Plains
Central Plains
Southern Plains

SARCEE

PLAINS CREE

BLACKFOOT

ASSINIBOINE

YAKIMA

NEZ PERCE

FLATHEAD

MANDAN

CROW

SIOUX

SHOSHONI

CHEYENNE

PAWNEE

ARAPAHO

SOUTHERN CHEYENNE

KIOWA

COMANCHE

PEOPLES OF THE PLAINS

Map of the Plains: Delineations include areas by Clothing Similarity and by Selected Tribes.

CHAPTER 1 - HEADING IN THE RIGHT DIRECTION

The Plains by Clothing Type

In this chapter we have included a color-coded map of the Plains that shows the three areas we have designated along with a number of tribes in each area. Others have divided what we identify as the "Northern Plains/Plateau" into Northern Plains, Plateau, Basin, and Inter-Montaigne, but for our purposes our simpler approach is more suitable. Note that we have not, by far, included all the tribes in each area. We did this to keep the map more readable.

There is a complexity in all three Plains areas that we do not show. Because this book is not an academically oriented ethnological treatise we have chosen

this simpler approach. However, we do acknowledge that our descriptions are considerably simplified.

Outfits in the three Plains Areas are distinguished by differences in the basic components: Hair Styles, Beadwork, Leggings, Breastplates, Moccasins, and Headdresses (See the chart below.). In addition, the Dancers of each area are quite distinctive. The chart below will allow the reader to do a quick comparison in each category. Thus, for example, one can see how hairstyles vary in the Central, Northern Plains/Plateau, and Southern by scanning from left to right in that section of the chart. This can be done in each category and cross-referenced to other relevant sections in this book.

GENERAL COMPARISON CHART FOR SELECTED PLAINS STYLES		
Central Plains	Northern Plains/Plateau	Southern Plains
<u>Hair Styles</u> Moderate braid length Parted in middle or side Worn loose when dancing	<u>Hair Styles</u> Medium braids Pompadour	<u>Hair Styles</u> Long braids Parted in middle Elaborate braid wraps
<u>Beadwork Style</u> Geometrical Lazy Stitch	<u>Beadwork Style</u> Geometrical & floral Lazy Stitch Crow Stitch Applique	<u>Beadwork Style</u> Geometrical & floral Lazy Stitch Applique
<u>Leggings</u> Cloth-single fold Buckskin-flap & fringe	<u>Leggings</u> Cloth-panel style Blanket	<u>Leggings</u> Cloth-single fold Buckskin-side tab
<u>Breastplates</u> Mostly 2-3 bones wide	<u>Breastplates</u> Mostly loop-style Some 2 bones wide	<u>Breastplates</u> Mostly 4 bones wide
<u>Moccasins</u> Hardsole Mostly low top Mostly fully-beaded uppers	<u>Moccasins</u> Hard- & Soft-sole Mostly high top Fully- & partially-beaded uppers	<u>Moccasins</u> Hardsole Low top Low top with/without flaps Fully- & partially-beaded uppers Vamp and heel fringe
<u>Headdresses</u> Coup feathers Warbonnets Roaches/2 feathers	<u>Headdresses</u> Coup feathers Warbonnets Roaches/no feathers Hair extenders	<u>Headdresses</u> Otter turbins Warbonnets Roaches/1 feather Hairplates
<u>Dancers' Wear</u> Mostly union suits Some with shirts and leggings Bustles on most dancers	<u>Dancers' Wear</u> 50% with shirts and bare legs 50% with shirts and leggings Some bustles	<u>Dancers' Wear</u> Mostly shirts and leggings Some with bare torso/legs Very few bustles

How to Do Research

It is our intent to illustrate beginning and intermediate outfits that can be directly copied from this book for those getting started. However, for the advanced craftsman who wishes to go beyond what is illustrated here, we want to describe the research techniques we use in order to be accurate in the re-creation of vintage outfits and items. The two methods we use will serve the advanced craftsman well and are described below.

Photography took root on the American scene around 1850. It became clear to the pioneers in the field that there was supreme value in using this new technology that superseded portraits and landscapes: the recording of historically important information. Perhaps the best-known early historical photographer who recognized this was Mathew Brady. His photographs of the Civil War are an invaluable record of our national history. Not long after Brady's efforts a number of photographers began recording images of Indians all across America. It is likely that the most famous of these men was Edward Curtis. His images are both historically and artistically important.

There were other photographers, less famous but equally important from an historical perspective.

Their photos can all serve as sources of information for the craftsman. It should be noted that the most useful photographs are those taken during the course of actual events; for example, photos taken at dances, of delegations in Washington, DC, and photos taken at other official events.

There are some limitations of vintage photography that need to be delineated:

(1) Perhaps the most important limitation is to note that some photographs, commonly referred to as studio photographs, were taken in staged settings. They are obviously posed and frequently feature items of dress that belonged to the photographer but not the Indian who is posing for the photograph. Thus, there could be the inherent flaw of mixing tribes and cultures. Any use of studio photographs should be further validated with other sources of evidence.

(2) A second limitation is due to the nature of film. We will not dwell on technical differences in films, but will just note that different types of film have different sensitivities to color. For example, red is reproduced as black and yellow is reproduced as white. Thus, it is nearly impossible to define the colors in a black and white photograph.

Shoshone man wearing a splithorn bonnet.
Curtis photograph ca. 1900

This splithorn bonnet was on display in the 1980's at the Heye Foundation Museum in New York City.

This reproduction splithorn bonnet can be seen in the Northern Plains/Plateau section on Intermediate Outfit Four.

This ledger art drawing by the artist, Pah-bo, is from Kiowa Memories by Ronald McCoy. A Southern Plains paddle-shaped headdress can be seen in this drawing.

A paddle-shaped headdress from the Smithsonian Institution's collection can be seen in The Plains Indians by Colin Taylor.

Our reproduction of the paddle-shaped headdress can be found in the Southern Plains section on Intermediate Outfit Four. It is worn in combination with a Double Feather Vertical Rig.

(3) At times photographers use filters that also alter contrast and color. This, too, makes identifying colors from black and white photographs an impossible task.

This, then, brings us to the second step in re-creating an object. Once an item or pattern is identified in a vintage black and white photograph, the colors are established by using era-correct museum exhibits, pieces from private collections, and color photographs from magazines or books. A typical example is illustrated in this section.

The example we show here is a splithorn bonnet typical of the Northern Plains/Plateau. The photograph of a Shoshoni man wearing a splithorn bonnet was taken by Curtis ca. 1900. The color photograph is from a Heye Foundation exhibit. These two images were used to create the design for the splithorn bonnet made for this book.

Another invaluable period resource is vintage ledger art. These are drawings made by Indians using discarded paper, much of it from ledgers. There are some limitations associated with this technique,

too: (1) The palette may have been limited by the pencil colors, crayon colors, or watercolors that were available to the Indian artists. Thus, one has to be cautious in regard to colors. That said, the color combinations used in ledger art are probably an accurate reflection of tribal preferences for beadwork and other items.

(2) Art, by its very nature, is interpretive. Thus, vintage ledger art drawings may feature idealized or imaginative images. For the reasons stated above, we still must use the verification technique described for using black and white photographs: color images from more modern sources. We include a specific example here, a Kiowa headdress.

The ledger art shows a Southern Plains man wearing an interesting headdress. An example of such a headdress can be found in Colin Taylor's book, *The Plains Indians*. Finally, we show a re-creation of this type of headdress in the third photograph.

From the time of first contact, Indians and whites established a trading relationship. On the Plains, furs and hides were traded for guns, blankets, beads, brass, and other manufactured goods.

Where to Find Materials

Research is preparation for making an outfit, but once the research is underway, locating the materials needed for projects looms large. Indians have been trading with commercial entities since the 17th Century. The businesses became much more institutionalized with the advent of trading posts. As seen in the painting above, they became a focal point for both business and social activities such as exchanging news and gossip. In this section we discuss the many modern sources of materials and tools. And there are many. For the beginning outfits described in this book, local shops may have all the materials and tools needed. However, eventually, you will need to buy items, which are only available through shops and trading posts that specialize in Indian-crafts. In the discussion that follows we will identify most of the sources you will need.

Fabric stores can supply you with cotton, calico, wool, canvas, bias tape, ribbons, needles and thread.

Beyond those items, they will probably sell fake fur, fabric dyes, fringe and sequins.

Craft stores can be expected to sell feathers, fluffs, bells, large beads, leather lacing, and other materials that can prove useful. Note that some fabric stores have craft sections with the same list of materials.

Some of the most useful sources of materials are thrift shops. Many of the outfits shown in this book use commercial vests, shirts, and silk scarves, all of which are commonly available at thrift shops. These shops can also be good sources of high quality dark red or blue wool: just look for large coats, and other items. Old belts can be used for mounting bells. Boots, jackets, and large purses can be very cost effective sources for certain kinds of leather. Thrift shops are not the only source of such items. Flea markets can offer an abundance of useful things. Antique shops are also worth visiting, but the prices might be in the out-of-budget range.

Central Plains Beginning Outfit Two with a bustle. Note that this outfit was completely constructed from items purchased at a local craft store and a local fabric store. The feathers in the bustle are turkey and duck, dyed black. The trailers are canvas; the spikes are dowels wrapped with imitation fur; the natural colored feathers are pheasant.

Southern Plains Intermediate Outfit Six with a bustle. This outfit, except for the moccasins, was completely constructed from items purchased from a mail order supply house. The bustle was made employing exactly the same patterns and techniques as the bustle in the photo on the left, but with imitation raptor feathers, real otter fur, and real elk hide.

Of course, local hardware stores are an obvious choice for tools. However, they are also a source for brass tacks, brass rings, wire, light chain and sheet brass. Wooden dowels and tool handles can be used to duplicate vintage items.

In some areas there are specialty leather craft stores. These stores will have belting leather, saddle leather, and commercial hides such as buckskin, split cowhide, sheepskin, and white rabbit. It is also possible that they sell metal conchos, brass spots and commercially beaded strips. Tools such as punches and leather scissors can be purchased there as well. Finally, some locales will have saddle shops with good sources of leather. Both leather shops and saddle shops often sell bundles of scrap leather that can be of use to a craftsman.

Whilst all these local shops are a bounty to the craftsman, probably the only place you will be able to find many of the needed materials are trading posts. Most do mail order business and produce annual catalogs that are resplendent with color photos of everything that is offered for sale. Perhaps the best way to describe these catalogs is to use a contemporary popular term: eye candy! The list of items available through these modern versions of the traditional Indian Territory Trading Post is so long that it cannot be conveniently described in detail here. However, a partial list includes: tanned hides of all sorts, rawhide, furs, feathers and fluffs, beads,

horns, claws, blankets, books, CDs, and on and on and on. Beyond these materials are many reproduction items such as bells made of both brass and chrome, selvedge-edge tradecloth, tomahawks and beadwork. There can also be finished items such as roaches, shirts, sashes, and moccasins.

Most Indiancraft-related mail order businesses are conveniently accessed via the Internet. Probably the best way to find them is to use a search engine such as Google. Thus, for example, one can Google "ermine skins" and find a number of businesses that supply ermine skins (hides) as well as other hides and furs. The Internet is a powerful tool for accessing shops and for getting information about nearly every Indiancraft subject one can imagine. A word of warning is mandatory: just because a business advertises on the Internet does not mean it is reliable. Some checking is required. Also, information regarding outfit design and construction found on the Internet may not be up to standard. All information gathered on the Internet needs to be verified. One example that exemplifies the need to verify is that of breastplates/bone hair pipes: vintage breastplates were made of natural bone and, thus, were whitish. However, a number of suppliers and craftsmen offer breastplates and/or bone hairpipes that are colored brown, black, red, etc. These would not be appropriate for any of the outfits discussed in this book.

Pages from a Crazy Crow Trading Post catalog. Note the great variety of goods and the color photographs of the items offered. This type of trading post may be the only source of needed materials.

16

Four photographs showing progression of a Plateau Outfit.

Progression

The next issue we need to discuss is progression. If you make a beginning item well, it can be used with Intermediate or Advanced Outfits. Thus, a nice set of beginning leggings can become intermediate by adding the correct commercial beadwork; they can become advanced by adding the proper hand-made beadwork. This is progression: improving an item or an outfit by changes and additions in a stepwise manner.

Consider the outfits in the four photographs above. The first photo shows a beginning Northern Plains/Plateau outfit. The second shows how to turn it into an Intermediate Outfit by adding kit-based accessories. The third shows how it can be made into an even better Intermediate Outfit by adding commercial beadwork, ribbons, and some additional enhancements. The fourth shows how it can be transformed into an Advanced Outfit by adding hand-made beadwork and other more advanced components. Thus, the photographs above show how a beginning Northern Plains/Plateau outfit progresses to intermediate and then to advanced by such additions.

The benefit of progression is that, by using the technique, you do not have to start from scratch each time you want to make improvements. Aprons illustrate what we mean. Note the aprons in each of the progression photographs: the basic apron used for the Beginning and Intermediate Outfits in the first two photographs is a simple wool rectangle with ribbon edging; the aprons used for the Intermediate and Advanced Outfits in the second two photographs are made from the same wool rectangle with ribbons, fake coins, and sequins added. These additions lend a completely different and much enhanced look to the outfits.

Craftsmanship

The essence of craftsmanship is to make something that looks right and is sturdy enough to be used for what it is intended. Beginners are often intimidated by the complicated appearance of a craft item and a lack of knowledge about details of the materials involved and the techniques needed.

It turns out that "complex" is not equal to "complicated". Complex just means that a series of simple steps is needed to complete the project. Complicated means that something is difficult to make. Most Indiancraft items are just complex, not complicated.

So, for example, in this book we describe how to make a set of aprons and a pair of leggings. They might look complicated to a beginner, but they are really quite easy to make. We would like to borrow a line from a famous shoe manufacturer: "Just Do It" and encourage you to just give it a try. Aprons and leggings are so basic to most outfits that they represent a good place to get started. The materials are very straightforward and can be found in any fabric store. Buy the needed materials and get whatever help you need for the sewing and just give it a try. We think you will be surprised at how easy it is.

CHAPTER 2 - "THE OUTFITS"

In each section we will start with beginning outfits and progress to intermediate and advanced outfits. The complete outfits have been photographed on mannequins. We have used neutrally colored mannequins and a neutrally colored background in order to focus attentio on the outfits rather than on the model. In addition we have included close-up photographs of the outfits and close-up photographs of many of the individual components. In this latter set of photographs of individual items we will provide some annotation that will assist the craftsman in either making or purchasing the item.

We have created the beginning outfits because we wanted to encourage you to get started by making authentic-looking (The Look) outfits so simple to assemble that they present almost no barriers at all.

The second grouping is intermediate and can be made by improving on the beginning outfits. In general, the intermediate outfits will feature bead work and other enhancements that can be either made by the craftsman or commercially purchased. The intermediate outfits may also require materials that are sold by specialty suppliers such as trading posts.

The third grouping, advanced outfits, require advanced skills such as beadwork and quillwork. They will also require materials that are sold by trading posts, fur and hide suppliers, and other specialty shops. It was not our intent to focus on the advanced outfits because this book is, in the main, directed at beginning and intermediate craftsmen. However, it is our hope that the advanced outfits will inspire the readers to progressively improve their outfits as they improve their skills.

It should be noted that the process of progression could improve upon any outfit. For example, the leggings on a beginning outfit can be enhanced with beadwork, thus, making them intermediate leggings. In reality, an outfit can consist of beginning, intermediate, and advanced components as the craftsman improves upon it.

Beginning

Intermediate

Advanced

This book gives instructions for simple headdresses, aprons, and leggings. We suggest using deck shoes as moccasin substitutes for Beginning Outfits.

The Basic Components

Two of the most difficult items for beginning crafts-men are headdresses and footwear. For headdresses we have included a section on the making of simple, but authentically styled, feather arrangements. For footwear, we show how to make substitute moccasins from readily available deck shoes.

Vintage outfits featured breechclouts, but sometime around the middle of the 20th Century aprons began to be used. We use aprons for our outfits because they are easy to make, resemble breechclouts suf-ficiently closely, are easier to use, and require less cloth and tailoring. It is mandatory to use a bathing suit or athletic shorts when wearing aprons and our mannequins are dressed in that manner. We include a section on making aprons and show how a simple, basic apron can be upgraded using progressively more elaborate trim.

Finally, many outfits utilized leggings. This type of leg-wear is very easy to make and can be enhanced. Thus, we have included a section that shows how to make simple leggings. In the Outfit Chapter we show how to enhance them in both intermediate and advanced fashion.

RICKMAN '12

Central Plains Outfits

In this section we describe outfits that were, mainly, used by the Sioux. Please note that we have adhered to our standard format: all outfits utilize athletic shorts and some type of footwear. Occasionally, the footwear will be hidden, though. As we have done in the other sections, we start with beginning outfits and progress to advanced outfits.

Finally, a word about bustles is in order. In the early days of the dance, bustles were limited to a few special dancers. However, with time, they became standard for all dancers. Because bustles require considerable craftsmanship, we have created a few outfits that do not have them. Except for fully formal outfits, bustles are truly mandatory for Intermediate and Advanced Central Plains dancers.

Beginning Outfit One

This is a basic dance outfit as seen ca. 1870-1890 at wardances and serves as the basis for other Central Plains dance outfits. Dance Outfits became more complex as wardances became more popular. The components of this one are a simple feather headdress referred to as a cluster, fake fur choker, plastic Crow bead bandolier, armbands made from tin cans, basic aprons, bells, fake fur anklets, and undecorated deck shoes.

The outfit can be used in its simplest form. However, it can be enhanced by using long johns: see Intermediate Outfit Two.

A cluster headdress; see Chapter 4, page 81 for assembly instructions.

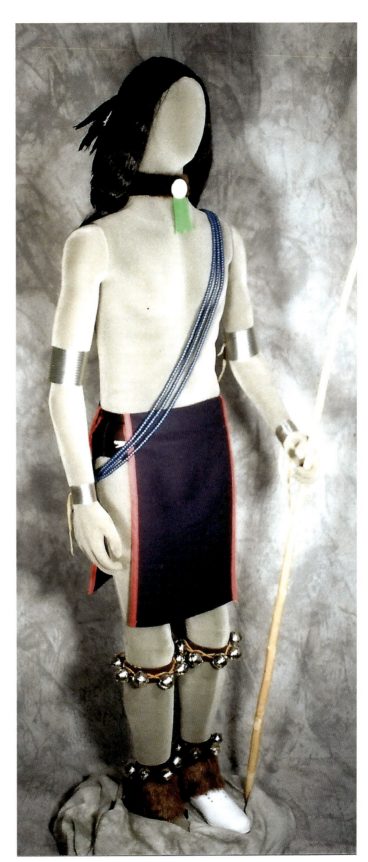

This is the basic Central Plains Dance Outfit, a good place to start.

Beginning Outfit Two

This outfit utilizes many of the components of Beginning Outfit One, but offers some nice enhancements. The most outstanding additions are the fake fur otter breastplate, the silk scarf, and aprons with enhanced ribbons.

Otter breastplates were often made from a complete otter hide, including the tail. Some were very plain, but others were decorated with ribbons and circular mirrors. The one shown here was made from fake otter fur, a standard item in most fabric stores. This fake fur is made so well that it is nearly impossible to distinguish from the real fur at even short distances. We recommend it highly.

The apron set features a front apron with parallel rows of ribbons that have been sewn on. The back apron remains very simple.

Modest additions to the basic outfit significantly improve its appearance.

The back of the outfit, showing the otter tail and the apron.

Beginning Outfit Three

This is a formal outfit rather than a dancer's outfit and serves as the basis for other Central Plains formal outfits. It, too, is typical for the 1870-1890 period. Note that it uses many of the components of Beginning Outfit One. However, the addition of a commercial shirt and simple leggings puts it in the category of a formal outfit.

Commercial shirts were often worn on formal occasions by Plains Indians and can be seen in numerous vintage photographs. Of course, they were typical of the shirts of that era in that they did not have collars. Note that such shirts were worn with leggings and not used on outfits that featured either bare legs or long johns.

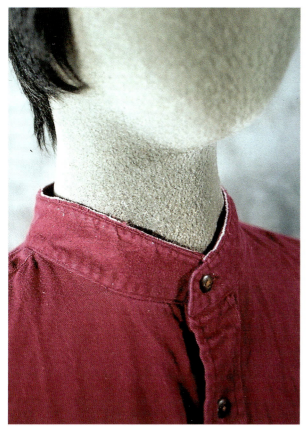

Note that the collar has been trimmed off a modern shirt in order to make it resemble a vintage shirt.

The addition of leggings and a commercial shirt make this outfit suitable for formal occasions.

An authentic look can be achieved on a budget.

Intermediate Outfit One

This basic outfit is more complex than the Beginning Outfits and is formal. It is comprised of a number of elements not seen in the beginning outfits.

Commercial vests were very popular items of dress for Plains Indians. They were commonly worn with a commercial shirt and leggings made of either hide or cloth. In fact, there are numerous photographs of Indian delegations to Washington, D.C. during the late 1800's in which many tribe members were dressed this way (See Page 2 for a circa 1875 photo of a Sioux delegation. All of the vests look new and none have been decorated yet.)

The leggings shown here are modeled on hide Flap-and-Fringe Leggings, but are made of canvas, which has been dyed. They have been further enhanced using iron-on tape to simulate beadwork. While this outfit has The Look, it is very inexpensive to make. We suggest that the reader compare this to Advanced Outfit Four in which many of the same components are used, but are made from more authentic materials. This comparison should serve to convince the reader that Intermediate Outfits, if made well, compare quite favorably to Advanced Outfits.

Painted deck shoes compare favorably to real beaded moccasins.

Intermediate Outfit Two

Intermediate Outfits require more craftsmanship and more specialized materials than do Beginning Outfits. This outfit is for a dancer and is very typical of Sioux dancers from about 1890 to as late as the 1950s. Many of the elements of this outfit were made from kits: fiber roach, choker, breastplate, and bustle.

The headdress is a fiber roach. Authentic roaches were made from porcupine guard hair and dyed deer tail hair. The roach is further decorated with a spreader and roach feathers. See pages 92-95. The dancer's neck features both a choker and a silk scarf. Also suspended from the neck is a breastplate. His armbands are made of belt leather and conchos.

The dancer is wearing a union suit (also called long johns) that has been dyed light red. Sometime around the turn of the century, Sioux dancers began to wear union suits that were white or dyed blue, red, yellow, purple, or green.

The dancer is wearing a fake otter fur breastplate worn like a bandolier. The breastplate is handsomely decorated with circular mirrors and painted quilled wheels.

Virtually all Sioux dancers of this period wore bustles. The one shown here is made of imitation golden eagle, and other dyed turkey feathers. The outfit is completed with bells and fake fur anklets.

Otter breastplates can be worn as bandoliers as well as over both shoulders.

On this outfit the roach, choker, breastplate, and bustle are made from kits.

Intermediate Outfit Three

With this outfit we add yet another dimension: the use of commercial beadwork. Like Intermediate Outfit One, this outfit represents a large change compared to the Beginning Outfits. This outfit definitely has The Look but was created using entirely commercial beadwork.

The beadwork shown on this old time Sioux dancer's outfit is all commercially available.

The headdress of the dancer is an authentic porcupine hair roach, normally referred to as a porky roach. The roach also features a spreader and roach feathers. This type of porky roach can be purchased from a number of trading posts.

The dancer's neck is decorated with both a silk scarf and real fur choker. Also suspended from the neck is a breastplate that is described in more detail below. This type of breastplate is not available in kit form and must be designed by the craftsman who, then, must obtain the correct materials in order to assemble it. The fan in the dancer's hand appears to be an eagle wing, but it was made from a perfectly legal goose wing.

Using long johns, as described previously, has enhanced the outfit.

The aprons are adorned with ribbons and decorative brass coins. The bells also merit special note. This probably represents one of the largest ensembles of bells a dancer would wear. They can be made from kits or designed and assembled from scratch.

The bustle is a classic design and was made using pheasant feathers. These bustles began to appear on dancers around ca. 1910. They are wonderful additions to an outfit—even an advanced outfit—but unfortunately there are no kits on the market presently. There are instructions for making them in out-of-print literature. Thus, this is a research project for the craftsman.

This ready-made roach and painted feathers were purchased from a mail order trading post.

The beadwork on this dancer is all commercial and can be seen in more detail in the photos below. The armbands and cuffs have been made by applying loom beaded commercial beadwork to hide bases. Since authentic beadwork would use the lazy stitch technique, this approach is not considered advanced. The pipebag is made in the same manner with a panel of simulated porcupine quillwork added to it. The beadwork on the moccasins are lazy stitched panels sold by trading posts. These have been attached to a pair of plain moccasins, as described below for the other beadwork examples.

The breastplate shown in these photos is decorated with commercially available, lazy stitch rosettes. Suspended from the rosettes are buckskin drops that have been painted with marking pens to make them look as if they have been wrapped with dyed porcupine quills. The drops end with tin cones that hold fluffs.

Commercial beadwork has been used extensively for this outfit. It is attached by using a thin coat of Aileen's Fast Grab Tacky Glue on the hide and, then, securing the edges by sewing. The simulated quillwork is made with a plastic panel which substitutes for rawhide, the normal base. Strips have been cut out of the panel and they have been wrapped with colored embroidery floss.

Pheasant bustles are an excellent alternative to imitation eagle feather bustles for the Central Plains.

Commercial beadwork, carefully selected, can represent your chosen tribe and time period. Attention to detail is needed. For example, the designs on the two sides of a pipebag are different.

27

Intermediate Outfit Four

With this outfit we enter yet another new area: individually handcrafted beadwork and real quillwork. However, the remainder of the outfit consists of components mostly similar to those we have already seen. The headdress is a porky roach with the usual spreader and roach feathers. There is also a silk scarf, real otter fur breastplate decorated with circular mirrors, bone hairpipe breastplate, aprons decorated with ribbons, concho-decorated belt and drop, vintage brass cuffs, bells, and real skunk fur anklets. As with the other bustles, it is up to the craftsman to do some research.

This dancer wears armbands and moccasins that are beaded using the lazy stitch method, typical of the Central Plains. Armbands represent ideal projects for this skill level. They use simple design elements, they are small projects, and they greatly enhance an outfit. Fully beaded moccasins, on the other hand, are more suited to a craftsman with significant beadworking experience.

Real wrapped porcupine quillwork probably represents a true difference-maker in an outfit. The quillwork on this dancer is seen on his *wapegnaka* or bullstail attached to the bottom of his roach spreader. Like fully beaded moccasins this type of project is best suited for the most experienced intermediate craftsman.

Lazy stitch beadwork can be seen on the armbands and moccasins.

On the left we see the back of the outfit; hawk or owl feathers are rarely seen, but are appropriate for the trailers on a Central Plains bustle. On the right is a close-up of the quillwork wapegnaka.

Intermediate Outfit Five

At first glance this outfit looks like it could be a prototypical Advanced Outfit. However, let us take a closer look.

The choker is made of real otter fur, the shirt is commercial, and the aprons, although made of reproduction tradecloth, are undecorated, all rather standard for intermediate work. The vest is delightfully decorated with cowry shells, an excellent addition to either an Intermediate or Advanced Outfit. However, armbands and cuffs are commercial loom beaded, an Intermediate standard. The leggings have been decorated with commercially available lazy stitch beadwork strips and have been enhanced with some brass spots. The moccasins appear to be fully beaded from a distance, but, again, close inspection would reveal them to be made with commercial lazy stitch panels attached to plain moccasins as discussed earlier.

It should be noted that it is suitable as a dance outfit by adding a bustle. Without a bustle, it is more appropriate as a formal outfit.

We have added a warbonnet to this outfit, our first example of using such a headdress.

Since this is the first time we see a warbonnet on an outfit, it merits some discussion. Warbonnets are items of honor and they deserve respect and proper care. All warbonnets should be worn with pride and when not being worn, should be stored carefully in a proper container.

The wearing of a warbonnet and a bustle combination was often seen on the Central Plains.

This is another all-commercial beadwork outfit. A simpler four-feather rig takes the place of the warbonnet.

Intermediate Outfit Six

For this outfit we show only the head and torso. For the remainder an assortment of leggings, aprons, and moccasins would be appropriate.

Of note on this outfit is the headdress with its stripped feathers and real quillwork on the bullstail.

In addition, note the armbands done in lazy stitch with a classical Sioux Star design. There are also bandoliers made of bone hairpipes and brass beads. However, the most striking component is the bandolier made of dozens of deer toes. This requires considerable work and craftsmanship, but the look is a delight and the sound it makes during a dance is subtle and unique.

Bandoliers make a dramatic accessory. They vary in their complexity.

The wapegnaka headdress, an excellent alternative to the roach.

Intermediate Outfit Seven

This is the classic outfit worn at important occasions by men such as chiefs. However, it can be used in both ceremonies and dances. It may surprise some to read that it can be used for dance. It should be made clear that the outfit must be complete as shown and not fragmented. It would not be correct to wear a warbonnet with long johns, for example.

This warbonnet qualifies as intermediate because it has a loom-beaded browband. A more advanced browband would be made using lazy stitch beadwork. Whilst the scope of this book does not include the history of warbonnets, we note in this section and in the Northern Plains/Plateau section that the creation of the flared warbonnet, which has become the standard, is generally attributed to the Sioux and the Crow. Another striking component of this outfit is the warshirt. It should be noted that it is made of canvas, carefully dyed and painted to look very much like the hide shirts after which it was modeled. And, of course, in line with its Intermediate status are the commercial loom beaded shoulder and arm strips.

The leggings are made from simulated tradecloth and also feature the commercial loom beaded strips, the design of which can been seen in all three areas of the Plains. And the moccasins are Plains soft sole with previously described commercial lazy stitch panels that are glued on.

The choker and the plastic bone hairpipe breastplate fit nicely into an Intermediate Outfit, as well.

An intermediate canvas-based warshirt with commercial beadwork rivals the advanced buckskin and lazy stitch beadwork version.

This outfit has the classic look, in spite of the fact that it utilizes mostly commercial loom beadwork and substitute materials.

Advanced Outfit One

This dancer, too, wears dyed long johns, a ribbon-decorated apron, and a porky roach, as expected. Of course, his breastplate is made of real bone hairpipe and his anklets are made of real fur. The other components of his outfit bear further scrutiny. The roach feathers are decorated with real quillwork strips and ermine fur tips. His choker is made of a large conch shell disc and vintage brass beads, although reproduction beads would be satisfactory. Along with the choker is an authentic Peace Medal. Here, too, reproductions can be found that are virtually identical to the real item.

His armbands and cuffs use the correct lazy stitch technique, as do his moccasins. The moccasins feature an American flag motif, commonly used during this period—and still seen in modern Plains beadwork. In addition, the tab pipebag and the wristband on his quirt also feature an American flag motif. We should note at this point that Sioux dancers of this period rarely used matching components; that approach came much later. The flag motif used for this dancer is somewhat subtle and should not be considered a matching set.

We would like to single out the roach feathers for further comment. They are adorned with quilled rawhide strips, thin ermine strips, and very small fluffs. These decorations are only on one side of a feather (the outer side when still on the bird). Most roaches featured two feathers; very occasionally, one feather was used.

The color combinations in this outfit are very eye-catching.

Beadwork and quillwork, accurate in design and color, mark the advanced outfit.

Advanced Outfit Two

This dancer's outfit, like that of Advanced Outfit One, is made mostly of items we have discussed previously. There are two new items to highlight: wool leggings with lazy stitch beaded strips and an otter breastplate with a quillwork panel at the bottom.

This outfit is really a variant of Advanced Outfit One and demonstrates how a craftsman can create several outfits by simply interchanging appropriate components.

Here is a beaded wapegnaka headdress with a somewhat complex two-feather rig.

Several components transform a dancer's outfit into a formal outfit. Added are leggings, a commercial shirt, and a quilled otter breastplate.

Advanced Outfit Three

Most of the Advanced Outfits we show are typical of those used by many Sioux dancers from about 1890 to as late as the 1950s. Advanced Outfits demand a high level of craftsmanship and access to highly specialized materials for nearly every item created. To the extent possible, the Advanced Outfit should be nearly indistinguishable from an authentic one, save its age. We have seen many of the components of Advanced Outfit Three on Intermediate Outfits: long johns, porky hair roach with spreader and roach feathers, silk scarf, and a bustle. However, a number of items that look familiar are, in fact, somewhat different than those we have discussed earlier.

This dancer has an otter breastplate that is made from real otter fur. Its decorations are the typical circular metal-back mirrors and silk ribbons. Like the breastplate, the anklets, too, are made of real fur. Nearly hidden by the otter breastplate is a bone hairpipe breastplate.

 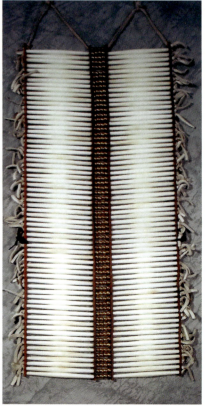

This dancer exhibits components that are almost standardized for an advanced, old time Sioux outfit.

Both full otter hides and bone hairpipe necklaces are called breastplates.

34

These types of breastplates, seen in photos here, were very typical of Old Time Sioux dancers and not seen anywhere else. It was very common for a dancer to sport both types in this manner. His armbands and cuffs have been made using lazy stitch beadwork, as have his fully beaded moccasins. His aprons are more highly decorated and probably represent the pinnacle of the craft. All of the Intermediate Outfits featured bells that had been chrome plated, completely authentic. However, because brass sleigh bells lend a special appearance to a dancer, we tend to think of them as an advanced component. They also are much more expensive.

The outfit is rounded out with two hand-held items: a classic warclub with a rawhide wrapped handle and a rope made of sweetgrass. With the exception of the imitation raptor feathers, every item on this outfit has been made with the same materials available to Indian craftsmen.

Typical accessories for this type of outfit include a concho belt with a drop club and a classic war club.

Central Plains mess bustles commonly feature spikes, a circle of feathers, an eagle tail, and feathered trailers.

Advanced Outfit Four

Here we see an Advanced Outfit featuring a warbonnet. This type of Outfit was commonly seen without a bustle, even at dances. Most of this outfit is comprised of components we have seen previously: real fur choker, commercial vest decorated with imitation elk teeth, commercial shirt, plain tradecloth aprons, and a beaded pipebag with a quillwork panel.

The different components are notable, however. The armbands are quillwork of standard design and color. The leggings are Flap-and-Fringe style made of real hide with real beadwork; the leggings of Intermediate Outfit One are modeled on this pair of leggings. The moccasins are partially beaded and partially quilled. The design is very typical of such moccasins.

We suggest that the reader compare this to Intermediate Outfit One in which many of the same components are used, but are made from more readily available and less expensive materials. This comparison should serve to convince the reader that there is a relationship between Beginning Outfits and Advanced Outfits and that relationship can be exploited as a craftsman improves his skills.

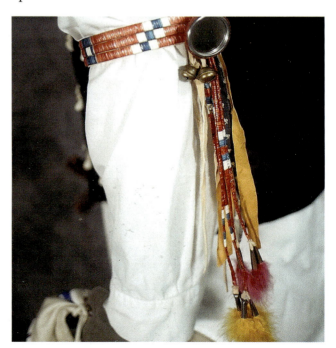

This type of outfit was worn by many delegates on diplomatic missions, as well as by dancers attending celebrations.

Armbands can be a good advanced quillwork project.

36

Advanced Outfit Five

This is our most formal Central Plains Advanced Outfit. The warbonnet is classic with its lazy stitch beadwork browband. The warshirt is decorated with quill-wrapped hair drops, along with lazy stitch beadwork arm and shoulder strips. The neck flap is also beaded with lazy stitch beadwork using a stylized American flag motif. The aprons are tradecloth, but with no decoration. The leggings are also made of tradecloth and have a classic, lazy stitch beadwork strip for decoration. The moccasins feature yet another style of buffalo hoof design. The outfit is finished with a pipebag featuring pictorial depictions of warriors on horseback.

This outfit has been made with careful attention to detail and the use of as much authentic materials and techniques as possible. It could easily be used as a museum exhibit.

Pictorial pipebags are a nice addition to an advanced outfit.

Outfits such as this, worn by important men, are elegant and are universally recognized as the epitome of American Indian dress.

Northern Plains / Plateau Outfits

In this section we describe outfits that are much more difficult to characterize by tribe than those in the Central and Southern Plains sections. Whilst the tribes of the Northern Plains/Plateau have created a quite distinct material culture, there is enough similarity to be able to combine them. For example, common to all are panel leggings, loop necklaces, and hairstyles. In addition, it is reasonable to sub-categorize these outfits by identifying them with three distinct tribes: Shoshone, Crow, or Blackfoot. However, as the craftsman becomes more sophisticated, he will have to be cognizant of the distinctions

and adhere much more carefully to specific guide-lines. We are painfully aware that we are engaging in oversimplification in this section, but it seems unavoidable. In part, the reason for this can be seen by looking at the tribal map of the area: there are many more tribes in the Northern area than in the other two.

A word about bustles is in order. Dancers on the Northern Plains/Plateau seemed to have limited bustles to a special group of dancers. In fact, bustles are truly an optional item for the Northern Plains/Plateau Dance Outfits shown here.

Beginning Outfit One

This Outfit can be thought of as being very typical of the Northern Plains/Plateau area and a good place to start. The necklace, made of plastic elk teeth and plastic discs, is a quite common design. Of course, the shirt and vest are commercial. Vintage ribbed armbands were usually made of brass. However, for this outfit they have been made by cutting portions from the ribbed section of a tin can and, thus, are chrome-toned.

Note the use of plaid material for the aprons. On the Plains, this approach was only used by the Northern tribes. The leggings, made from a kit, are specific to the Northern Plains/Plateau and we will see them throughout this section. They are called panel leggings in reference to the red panels that adorn the ankle area. Finally, undecorated deck shoes were used to simulate moccasins.

A simple looped end makes it easy to tie a coup feather into the hair.

The distinctive hairstyle, panel leggings, and plaid apron tell us that this is a Northern Plains/Plateau outfit.

The shirt and vest for this outfit were purchased at a thrift store; the blankets used to make the leggings and aprons were found at a flea market.

Beginning Outfit Two

This Outfit can also be thought of as being very typical of the Northern Plains/Plateau area. It appears to be elaborate but is comprised of easily made parts.

The necklaces are: a Peace Medal suspended on a ribbon, a choker consisting of two strands of brass beads, a strand of alternating white and red beads enhanced with some fake elk teeth, and a tanned ermine hide. The ermine hide could be simulated with some rabbit fur.

The shirt and vest are commercial. The aprons are made of sections of a wool blanket, which feature horizontal stripes. The leggings are panel style, made from a Hudson Bay-type blanket. Whilst blanket leggings were very common on the Northern Plains/Plateau, they were almost never seen on the Central or Southern Plains. The original blankets were wool and can still be purchased, but are fairly expensive. The leggings on this outfit were made from a Sears candy stripe blanket. And, as usual for a Beginning Outfit, we used deck shoes for moccasins.

Easily made accessories, using supplies purchased from a trading post, complete this outfit.

Beginning Outfit Three

Note that this is a dancer's Outfit, but without a headdress or bustle. This is perfectly acceptable for all the tribes and categories in this area. The shirt is commercial, but has been customized by cutting fringe at the sleeves. Bells have been slung over the shoulder, bandolier-style and is a trait specific to the Northern Plains/Plateau.

A breechclout has been used instead of aprons. It is decorated with ribbons of varying width, but special note should be taken of the backside. It is not a flap, but, instead, is a short section in which the ribbons are sewn on using a chevron pattern. That said, it would be acceptable to make a set of aprons with the backside decorated using a chevron pattern. The leggings are made of simulated selvedge edge trade-cloth. The design of the commercial loom beadwork is used across the Plains area.

The outfit is completed with soft sole moccasins decorated with a keyhole design made from a commercial rosette and a hand-beaded trapezoid.

Ribbons on the breechclout and the mountain design on the commercially beaded strips on the leggings add color to this outfit.

The bandolier for this dancer is simply a full set of vintage sleigh bells draped over one shoulder.

41

Intermediate Outfit One

This Outfit shows a Crow-style dancer. The headdress is a fiber roach kit. The kit necklace is common and specific to the Northern Plains/Plateau. It is called a loop necklace and can be made of a variety of materials. Regardless of the materials used, loop necklaces generally consist of about a dozen loops of increasing length attached to two parallel leather strips, two large shells tied about halfway along the leather strips, and long fringe adorning the outside of the parallel leather strips.

The upper arms, wrists and ankles feature fur bands, both fake and real. Simple aprons made of wool with ribbon edging have been used. Leg bells extend from the waist to the ankles and are terminated with an ankle bell set. The deck shoe moccasins have been enhanced by painting a typical Crow moccasin pattern on them.

This Outfit includes a bustle that uses the same kit feathers as Central Plains Intermediate Outfit Two, but in a Northern style. It consists of spikes, feathers attached to a base in shingle-like rows, and two trade cloth trailers with three rows of three imitation golden eagle feathers. While this bustle may appear complex, it is a fairly simple craft item and is perfectly suitable for an Intermediate Outfit.

The characteristic loop necklace tells us that this is a Northern Plains/Plateau dancer.

Spikes on this type of bustle do not point upward, but are almost horizontal to the ground.

Intermediate Outfit Two

This Outfit is for a Blackfoot-style dancer. The headdress is a porky roach and resin-based spreader purchased from a trading post. There are two necklaces: the first is a choker made of various colors of crow beads with a few brass beads; the second is a version of the standard loop necklace. This may be the simplest version as it is constructed of the usual parallel leather strips, loops of easy-to-obtain crow beads, and long strands of fringe.

The commercial shirt has been customized by cutting fringe in the sleeves. The armbands were made from tin cans. The commercial belt has been decorated with bells.

This dancer is carrying a pipebag made with commercial floral beadwork pieces and fringe decorated with tile beads.

Aprons have been used for this Outfit, but in a manner unique to the Northern Plains. Originally, the effect was achieved by hanging a breechclout over the front of the belt only. Thus, one could see the ribbon work on both the front and back of the breechclout when looking at only the front side of the dancer. The very same effect can be achieved using aprons as seen on this Outfit. Because both aprons have been suspended from the front, a bustle becomes important. This simple bustle consists of overlaying concentric circles of turkey and pheasant feathers with a trailer of imitation eagle feathers. The leggings are made from a special northern-style trade cloth, but with a novel fringe approach on the flaps. This is seen only on northern outfits. Bells at the knees and soft-soled moccasins finish the look.

Chevron-style ribbons on the apron, unique northern tradecloth, fringed sleeves, and a loop necklace all proclaim this to be a Northern outfit.

Pheasant, white turkey, natural grouse, and imitation eagle wing feathers comprise this Blackfoot-style bustle. Notice the absence of spikes.

This outfit takes advantage of commercially available, imported beadwork, which has been applied to blankets found at a flea market.

Intermediate Outfit Three

This Outfit is Shoshone-style and has been created using kits and many pieces of commercial beadwork. The headdress, called a splithorn bonnet, is made with steer horns cut very narrow, faux ermine fur (white rabbit), and a commercial beadwork browband. There are two kit necklaces: a choker and another variant of loop necklace. The shirt is commercial with armbands made from tin cans. The faux otter hide breastplate is worn bandolier style. The line of brass beads connecting the metal-backed mirrors is seen only in the Northern Plains/Plateau area. The wool blanket is decorated with commercially beaded blanket strips and rosettes. The aprons have been adorned with ribbons and brass sequins. The panels on the leggings were made using commercially available beaded floral pieces. The soft-soled moccasins were enhanced with commercially beaded medallions.

Accessories such as this coup stick, the otter hide bandolier, and the horn warclub were created from locally found materials in combination with trading post supplies.

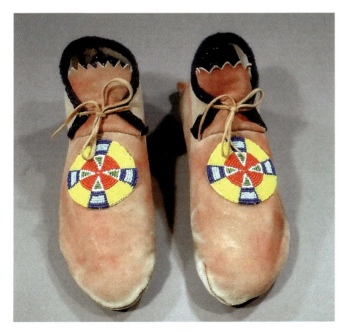

The splithorn bonnet, loop necklace, and soft sole moccasins were made using somewhat modified trading post kits.

You should be conscious of how the back of your outfit looks. It should be as complete and pleasing as the front.

Intermediate Outfit Four

This Outfit is a Crow-style Dance Outfit and is notable due the complete absence of beadwork. In addition, it can be used as a Formal Outfit by simply removing the bells. Similar to Intermediate Outfit Three, it features a splithorn bonnet made with a split, cut-down steer horn (but now painted black) faux ermine fur (white rabbit), and a browband (not beaded, but made of red wool and hawk bells). The three necklaces consist of a simple string of glass beads; a string of brass beads with a large shell disc; and a hide leather lacing with various feathers, beads, hawk bells, and a buckskin medicine bag suspended from it. The shirt is commercial: the front opening was sewn together; it was dyed at the shoulders, waist, and sleeves, and, finally, fringed at both the waist and sleeves. The aprons are made from green selvedge edge trade cloth. Finally, there are ankle bells and Plains soft-soled moccasins with high tops.

On the Northern Plains and Plateau areas you often see dancers wearing a shirt, but with bare legs. Less often you see dancers with leggings and a bare torso.

Fringed cloth shirts, with or without dyed fringes, are quite common on the Northern Plains and Plateau areas. Splithorn bonnets are also commonly seen.

Intermediate Outfit Five

This Outfit can be considered Blackfoot-style. The porky roach has no feather. The dancer's hair has been enhanced with an extender made of black braids, ermine mini-wraps, and a beaded panel with medallions at each end. A hair extender is often worn with a modern haircut. It gives one instant hair-length and a pair of braids. A thin leather tie acts as a headband and the ends of the leather lacing form a nice drop. There are two necklaces: one is a choker-type, made of tubes and brass beads; the second is another variety of loop necklace. This is made by wrapping seed beads around rope loops. No shirt is needed with the commercial vest. The armbands and wristbands are made of brass, but ones made from tin cans can be used. The aprons (not visible) are made of selvedge edge trade cloth. There are bells at the knees and ankles along with soft-soled moccasins.

A rather large bustle consists of long decorated spikes, numerous concentric circles of whole and stripped feathers, a tail of imitation golden eagle feathers, and a pair of trailers featuring natural dark turkey feathers.

Some northern dancers wear neither leggings nor a shirt. Instead, they put on a decorated vest over their bare torso.

Hair extenders were favored on the Northern Plains and Plateau areas. The style seen here can be considered Blackfoot with its thin separated braids and beaded band with rosettes. A few glass and brass beads below the headband knot create a nice drop.

Intermediate Outfit Six

This Crow-style Formal Outfit features a classic flared warbonnet with a shingled fur-covered cap. The warshirt is made of hide, but the beadwork is commercial. The bibs are handmade using the lazy stitch method, with beads selected to match the commercial strips. We considered this project to be within the capability of an intermediate craftsman. The aprons are typical selvedge edge trade cloth. The panel leggings feature handmade beadwork that should also be within the capability of an intermediate craftsman. The moccasins, at first glance, would appear to be beaded and well beyond the capability of an intermediate craftsman. However, the beadwork consists of commercial panels that may be purchased from trading posts and applied to moccasins with relative ease.

This outfit shows a blend of commercial and handcrafted beadwork. The shirt strips are imported loom beadwork, but the shirt's bib and legging panels display the more accurate handcrafted lazy stitch.

The long imitation ermine bonnet drops and the shirt's dramatic sweeping imitation ermine tubes identify this outfit as a quintessential Northern Plains/Plateau formal outfit.

Advanced Outfit One

This is a Shoshone-style Formal Outfit. The headdress is made using a single feather rig with a counterweight consisting of a circular mirror, ermine skin, and a silk scarf. Two necklaces are seen on this outfit: a choker-type made from leather strips and tubes; and a very standard loop necklace, but without fringes. The shirt was made using a purchased pattern and is enhanced by the use of a bandolier made from leather strips, bone hairpipe, glass beads, and cowry shells. The panel belt holds a delightful pouch that has been fully beaded with floral appliqué.

The aprons continue the floral appliqué theme with a perfectly executed Northern Plains/Plateau design. The floral appliqué panels are authentic in design and construction. A nice finishing touch are the soft sole moccasins with the floral appliqué vamps.

Here we see a fully floral applique beaded pouch mounted on a lazy stitched panel belt. The soft sole moccasins feature floral applique on the vamps.

The handcrafted floral applique beadwork displayed on this outfit indicates countless hours of research and a mastery of the art form.

The front and back panel designs on the leggings use the red wool as a background color, whilst the apron uses the blue wool in the same manner.

Shirts made of muslin cloth were quite popular on the Northern Plains and Plateau areas. They are an authentic substitute for the traditional heavy buckskin warshirt.

Advanced Outfit Two

This is another Crow-style Dance Outfit. The headdress is a simple feather rig, but the hairstyle is a pompadour. As with most Northern Plains/Plateau area dancers, the necklace is loop style. The outfit also features a muslin shirt with beaded red wool epaulets and red wool welting in the seams. The sleeves and bottom of the shirt have wide fringe, which can be left plain or dyed red.

The aprons are wide ribbon- and brass sequin- decorated trade cloth. Ankle bells, soft sole moccasins, and a bustle complete the outfit. While we have stated that a bustle is optional for a Northern Plains/Plateau dancer, a simple outfit such as this is served well with one.

It is not necessary for an outfit to have a profusion of beadwork to be advanced. The sparse beadwork on the shirt's epaulets is sufficient for this outfit. However, the fully beaded mirrorbag is an elegant addition.

Advanced Outfit Three

This is a Crow-style Dance Outfit. The headdress is a porky roach with a rawhide spreader and turkey leg bone sockets. The feathers are imitation eagle with small ermine strips and hair at the tips. The only necklace is a loop-type. The dancer wears no shirt and has brass wristbands. The armbands are quite unusual and seem to be limited to Crow dancers, as are the rectangular mirror bags. The unique armbands are made from the lower leg of a deer and still have the hooves and dewclaws attached. They are lined with red wool that also serves as drops.

The aprons are wide selvedge edge trade cloth. Leg bells, knee bells, soft sole moccasins, and a bustle complete the outfit. While we have stated that a bustle is optional for a Northern Plains/ Plateau dancer, this outfit would be rather barren were it not for the bustle and we would recommend one in this case. The bustle shown is very complex and is comprised of nearly every component one would see on a bustle: spikes, numerous concentric circles of whole stripped and dyed feathers, and two trailers--each with four rows of three imitation eagle feathers.

The deer hoof armbands identify this outfit as uniquely Crow.

This simple loop necklace is a classic.

This dance outfit represents a traditional old time Crow dancer of the late 19th Century.

51

Advanced Outfit Four

This Outfit is a Shoshone-style Formal Outfit. The headdress is a splithorn bonnet made with split, trimmed and bent buffalo horn. The covering and drop tubes are all real ermine. The beadwork is hand-crafted lazy stitch. Two necklaces are seen: one is a choker-type made of glass beads and brass beads; the second is a loop necklace made with parallel leather strips, loops of seed bead-wrapped beadwork, and fringes. The old style drop shoulder shirt was made using a purchased pattern and is enhanced with brass armbands, floral-beaded cuffs, and a panel belt. The breechclout is fully decorated with ribbons, buttons, coins, brass sequins, and gold braid. The leggings used in conjunction with the breechclout are panel-style with beadwork on the panels. The partially beaded moccasins are Indian-made and were purchased.

Plateau outfits were often very colorful. Their breechclouts and aprons tended to be more heavily decorated than those of the Central Plains.

Bonnets featuring split horns had crowns covered with strips of ermine fur and supported trailers of ermine fur tubes or eagle feathers. In the old days the horns were mostly buffalo or elk, but more recently they were cow horns.

Advanced Outfit Five

This is one of the most elegant Old Time outfits created by the Crow. The viewer's eyes are drawn to it due to the dramatic contrast created by the colors of its components. This is seen in the juxtaposition of the brilliant light blue beadwork background against the white of the braintan of the warshirt, the way the beadwork and red wool of the panels stand out against the dark blue wool of the leggings, and the natural contrast of the black tips of the ermine tubes with the white of the body fur. The ermine tubes, in their parallel profusion, create much the same effect that matching black and white eagle feathers do in a warbonnet: they capture the eyes and will not let go.

Every component of this Advanced Outfit is as close to an original Old Time Crow outfit as is possible today.

The warshirt features a dramatic array of over 80 hand-stitched ermine tubes.

All the handcrafted beadwork lends authenticity to this outfit: applique and lazy stitch on the moccasins, lazy stitch on the legging panel, and applique and lazy stitch on the fan handle.

This formal Crow outfit features a warshirt made of braintan; handcrafted beadwork with traditional designs has been added to shoulders and sleeves.

Southern Plains Outfits

In this section we describe outfits of the Southern Plains. There are many tribes in this area whose names are well known to the general populace due to their heroics in the Indian Wars—and due to the magnificent art they created. This art was not expressed in outfits alone, but also on paper and canvas, as well as other media. Indeed, that creativity continues today and can be seen at powwows and in numerous museums and art collections. Whilst the list of notable tribes is long, due to our space limitations, we have had to narrow it to the group

represented by the Kiowa, Comanche, Arapaho, and Southern Cheyenne. Although most of the outfits might be considered generic Southern Plains, those of the Kiowa and Comanche most heavily influenced us.

The reader will notice that Southern Plains Outfits offer an interesting distinction; the majority feature leggings and, thus, can be used for either dance or formal occasions. If used for dance, one merely adds bells!

Beginning Outfit One

This Outfit and the other Beginning Southern Plains Outfits are all quite similar. They are the most basic of outfits and can be worn as shown, as well as serving as the basis for the more complex outfits. As with other Beginning Outfits in this book, they are notable due to how easy they were to assemble. Most of the components were either purchased at thrift stores or made with modest efforts. The components of Beginning Outfit One are: feather headdress, a single-strand choker made of brass- and blue-colored plastic Crow beads, a silk scarf, a two-strand bandolier made of brass-colored beads, fake wooden mescal beans, commercial white shirt and vest, basic narrow aprons, contrasting-in-color wool leggings, and undecorated deck shoes. The length and narrowness of the aprons is very characteristic of the Southern Plains; such aprons are rarely seen outside this cultural area.

Bandoliers often have a single scarf hanging at the back.

This simple headdress consists of a looped feather with light fixture chain drops suspended from a brass button.

This easily made beginning outfit features a red wool apron, which contrasts nicely with the dark blue wool leggings.

Beginning Outfit Two

As noted, this outfit utilizes components that are similar to Beginning Outfit One, but still features its own unique look. The headdress is still based on looped feathers with attendant decoration. Note that the aprons and leggings are still contrasting in color, but now the leggings are red and the aprons blue. Also note that the commercial shirt is colored. But, what seems to stand out are the braid wrappings. This look can be achieved using fake braids that attach to the hair. The contrasting diamond colors are achieved by crisscrossing two strips of wool during the wrapping process.

Commercial shirts and vests can be obtained at thrift stores and vintage clothing stores.

Beginning outfits one and two are basically the same, but the different colors of the components make each unique.

On the Southern Plains leggings, the tie ends hang on the front. Simple headdresses and drops, as well as colorful neckerchiefs and braidwraps, complete the outfit.

Intermediate Outfit One

For this category of outfits we limit the number of items requiring craftsmanship and we depend on commercially available items such as beaded medallions and metal conchos. However, the outfits are considerably enhanced when compared to those in the Beginning category. For Intermediate Outfit One we show only the upper body, but any combination of aprons and leggings used on the Beginning Outfits would work well here. Two items stand out, though: (1) the hair ornament which features commercial metal conchos and (2) the German silver pectoral. Both of these items can be purchased from trading posts, including on-line sites. Note also the two-color braid wrappings, somewhat similar to those on Beginning Outfit Two.

This mannequin wears a white man's haircut combined with fake braids attached to the back of the hair.

A single feather horizontal rig is covered by a three-inch diameter silver concho. The remaining conchos, descending in decreasing diameter, serve as a counterbalance.

Southern Plains outfits abound with silverwork. Above is a German silver pectoral, worn as a necklace, showing stamped and etched designs.

Intermediate Outfit Two

In order to demonstrate how versatile this outfit is we have shown it in three variations. All were created with the same base, but each used a different headdress, resulting in three quite distinctive looks.

Variation One features some very interesting components. Note the use of two different materials for the braid wraps, otter fur and diamond pattern-wrapped wool. Also note that the vest uses, in part, a US military motif. This too, is nearly unique to the Southern Plains and should be avoided when creating outfits for other cultural areas. Finally, note the use of a folded trade cloth blanket around the waist. This is not unique to the Southern Plains and could be used for a wide variety of outfits. Variation Two features the same basic outfit but with a fake otter fur turban. Otter turbans of this style were nearly unique to the Southern Plains. Variation Three also features the same basic outfit, but with a classic Southern Plains-style warbonnet.

When choosing colorful patterned shirts, keep in mind that Indian people also fancied wearing plaids.

Headdresses denote status. Ledger art indicates that coup feathers and hairplates were the most common headdresses worn on the Southern Plains. Otter caps and war bonnets seem to indicate men of a higher status.

Intermediate Outfit Three

This outfit is a considerably dramatic variation, but remains in the intermediate category. The enhancements are due, in the main, to the extensive use of commercial beadwork.

The headdress is a fake otter fur turban decorated with numerous commercial beaded medallions and a commercial loom beaded strip. In an authentic turban, the beading on the strip would normally be done using the appliqué method. Besides the beaded medallions on the turban, there are four on the otter fur braid wrappings. In addition to the otter braid wrappings, there is a breastplate made of plastic bone hairpipes and a two-strand bandolier made of fake mescal beans.

Commercial beadwork is also seen on the leggings. These strips are loom beaded, but in an authentic pair of leggings the beadwork would be done using the lazy stitch technique.

Research shows that Southern Plains otter turbans have varying numbers of rosettes.

These braid wraps are made of fake fur backed with yellow felt.

The beaded rosettes, legging strips, and moccasin tops are commercially imported beadwork.

Intermediate Outfit Four

In this Formal Outfit we can see several variations of items shown previously. We have done this to demonstrate, to a limited degree, that there is room for variation in a given item.

The breastplate, made of plastic bone hairpipes, consists of six columns of hairpipes and is specific to the Southern Plains. The leggings are made of canvas that has been dyed to resemble a yellow-painted hide. Of course, this is much less expensive than using real hide. The canvas was dyed with readily available RIT dye. All the beadwork is commercially available. Finally, the remaining components have been previously discussed, and the outfit may be converted to an Intermediate Dance Outfit by the addition of bells.

These yellow-dyed canvas flap-style leggings are a very good substitute for expensive buckskin.

The headdress is really only an elaborate two-feather vertical rig. The paddle covers the rig and the hairplates act as a counterbalance.

A hardware store chain suspended from a large brass button creates the drop that completes the headdress.

Intermediate Outfit Five

This outfit has some unique features that differentiate it from other similar-looking Intermediate Southern Plains Outfits. For example, we can see yet another version of the otter turban. In addition to the commercial beaded medallions, this turban also has a top band decoration consisting of a multicolored ribbon and brass sequins.

Another interesting variation is the attachment of the otter braid wraps. At first glance, it looks like they are attached to the hair. In fact, they are attached to the top of the breastplate. Also note the decoration at the ends of the wraps. Clearly, they can provide a nice focus on an outfit.

The choker is made from imported dentalium shells. The final addition to the neck area is a classic Southern Plains-style breastplate made of bone hairpipes, brass beads and glass beads. Since this is an Intermediate Outfit, plastic hairpipes would also be suitable.

The commercial vest is enhanced with brass spots at the armholes, a typical decoration used across the Plains. The German silver armbands are a nice touch. They can be purchased at many trading posts. The leggings and aprons are made of reproduction tradecloth and feature minimal decoration. As usual, this outfit can be used for dance by adding bells.

This otter turban features a multi-colored ribbon at the top, graduated commercial beaded rosettes, and a handcrafted beaded end on the tail.

These braidwraps are attached to the tops of the breastplate ties.

The pipebag is handcrafted, but the rosettes are all commercially beaded.

Intermediate Outfit Six

All the previously shown Intermediate Outfits could be used as either formal outfits or, with the addition of bells, converted to dance outfits. Intermediate Outfit Six is specifically a dance outfit. Around the late 1800's many dancers on the Southern Plains resembled the Central Plains dancers of that era. The major exception was the selvedge edge on the tradecloth; it was often rainbow instead of white. This outfit is such an example.

The headdress is a porky roach worn near the back of the head and features a single feather. The braids have not been wrapped. Further decoration includes a double-strand bandolier made using mescal beans. As mentioned, this dancer is meant to look like one from the late 1800s. Thus, he has no body covering as such, other than a set of aprons made from rainbow selvedge tradecloth. The outfit is rounded out with knee bells and Cheyenne-style moccasins.

Southern Plains men in standard dance outfits closely resembled Central Plains dancers. Subtle differences such as the use of mescal beans, yellow flicker feathers, and rainbow selvedge edged tradecloth identify this as a Southern Plains dancer.

Up until the early 20th Century when fluffy-style Fancy Dance bustles became popular, Southern Plains dancers used traditionally styled War Dance bustles.

Advanced Outfit One

With this outfit we make the leap to the advanced category. The changes are somewhat subtle. For example, real otter fur is used exclusively instead of fake fur. In addition, all of the metal hairplates were handcrafted and are not imported. Note also that the breastplate is made of real bone hairpipes and is decorated with an authentic Peace Medal and a vintage German silver pectoral.

The reader will have noted that Southern Plains Outfits feature considerable metalwork. Thus, on this outfit there are the following: German silver pectoral, earrings made of brass components, German silver drops on the scalp feather, and metal hair plates.

The tab leggings are made from hide and fit the advanced criteria since they are enhanced with beading on the tabs and twisted fringe below the tabs. In addition, they have been colored using earth-tone paint. Finally, the moccasins are the type referred to as dusters, a classic standard on the Southern Plains.

The sides of this looped coup feather have been trimmed and notched.

These side tab leggings have been painted with powdered earth pigments.

The vamps and tongues of these moccasins are also painted with earth pigments.

This four-row breastplate features both long and short bone hairpipes.

This outfit features the same components as many of the intermediate outfits. However, with the exception of the vest, all the components are handcrafted.

Advanced Outfit Two

With this advanced outfit we enter so much new territory that we will discuss each component in detail. In many ways this outfit and the one that follows represent the pinnacle of the genre.

The turban is made from a rich deep brown summer otter hide and is decorated with numerous beribboned-beaded medallions of classic design. The tail is completed with a peyote-beaded slide that houses a spectrum of colored ribbons.

The breastplate is made of real bone hairpipes of two different lengths and utilizes a herringbone pattern, typical of the Southern Plains. The addition of a nice German silver pectoral completes the breastplate. The outfit is further complemented with a three-strand bandolier of brass beads.

The aprons are made of ribbon-edged rainbow selvedge reproduction tradecloth. The tab leggings are made from braintan and have velveteen-lined tabs, the ends of which feature horsehair brushes encircled with peyote beadwork. Below the tabs are panels of twisted fringe. The ankle area is highlighted with lazy stitch beadwork, red-dyed panels, and flat fringe.

We also introduce, with this outfit, a traditional four-way rainbow selvedge edge reproduction tradecloth blanket with a classic lazy stitch beaded blanket strip consisting of both rectangular panels and lazy stitch medallions. This type of blanket is found throughout the Southern and Central Plains.

As elegant as this outfit is, the shirt and vest come from a thrift store and the simple quirt is made from a piece of wood molding.

The apron is rainbow selvedge edge wool tradecloth.

The pipebag is Southern Cheyenne-style with a military stripe motif.

The inside of the tabs are lined with velveteen cloth instead of being painted.

The rosettes on the turban and the beaded blanket strip require advanced craftsmanship.

Advanced Outfit Three

This is a second pinnacle of the classic Southern Plains look. The roach, made of horsehair (standard in many early roaches), has an elk antler spreader. The drop consists of a German silver panel-chain with a bear claw and a German silver crescent.

The piêce de rêsistance of this outfit must be the warshirt. It is constructed of commercially tanned sheep hide and festooned with dozens and dozens of twisted fringes at the bib, shoulders, and sleeves. An elegant touch is provided by the large size of the triangular bibs, painted red-orange and outlined with lazy stitch beadwork.

Whilst the breastplate is one of many standard patterns, note that it is constructed of long bone hairpipes that have been cut in half, a technique unique to the Southern Plains. The breastplate is made even more notable by the addition of a vintage pectoral of novel design. The breastplate is further enhanced by the presence of a two-strand bandolier of mescal beans and brass beads.

The bear claw adds drama to this drop.

A back view of the outfit shows the over-sized bib with fringe.

Simple otter braid wraps frame the breastplate and its unusual German silver pectoral.

This outfit includes a rare old style Southern Plains flat fan of imitation eagle tail feathers.

Worn on diplomatic missions, during ceremonies, and on special occasions, the full hide shirt and leggings provide stately attire.

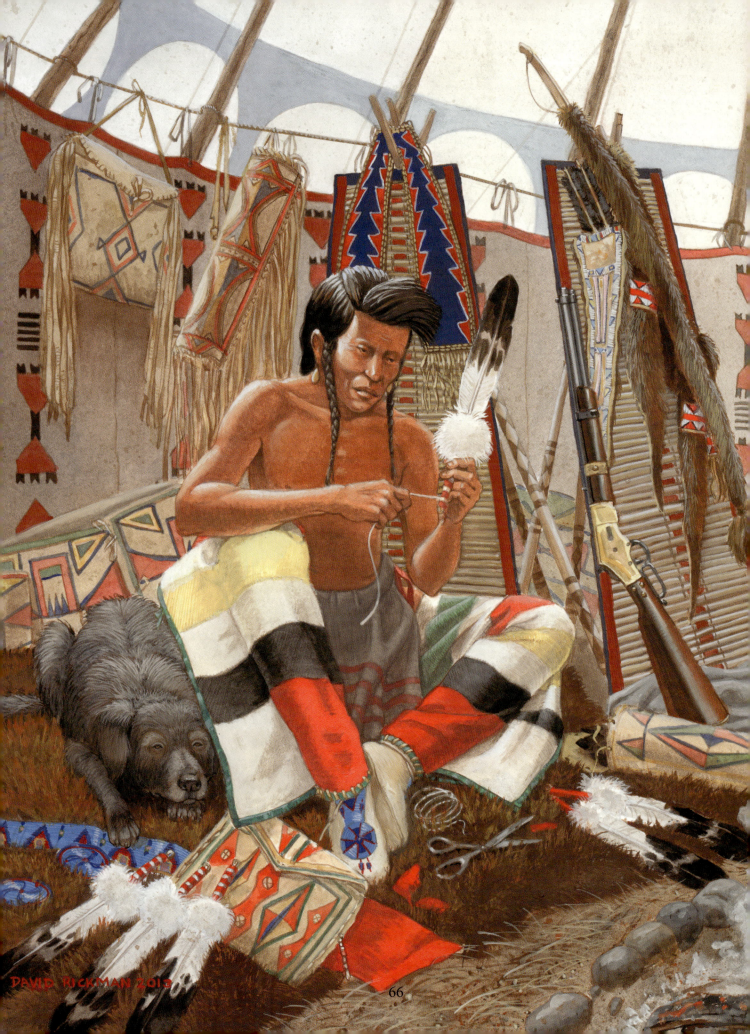

CHAPTER 3 - HOW TO MAKE IT
APRONS AND LEGGINGS

Breechclout or Aprons?

The most basic item of clothing for Plains Indian men was the breechclout. It was a single strip of hide or cloth that slid between the legs and was held on at the waist with some sort of belt. However, today's powwow dancers use a substitute: a pair of aprons along with athletic shorts. This combination is much more convenient and we recommend its adoption for the outfits we have described. Aprons are basically two flaps, one in front and one in the rear. Each apron has a loop sewn at the top into which the belt is inserted. The system is completed with a set of shorts or a bathing suit under the aprons. Aprons were rapidly adopted since they were easier to put on and were somewhat more modest. Because one can retain The Look and substitute aprons for a breechclout, we recommend this approach. For the sake of accuracy the text below will refer to breechclouts, but the reader can mentally substitute the word aprons.

For the period covered by this book, breechclouts were generally made from selvedge edge tradecloth. The white selvedge edge became part of the decoration of the breechclout, adorning the lower front and back edges. Early breechclouts tended to have very short flaps. With time the flaps became longer and were more highly decorated. Some breechclouts never had a flap on the back; there was just a loop into which the belt fit. This arrangement persisted well into the 20th century. In fact, if a bustle were worn, a back flap was nearly a nuisance. In general, we tend to favor making both a front and a rear flap for aprons. However, if you are wearing a large enough bustle, the rear flap can be optional.

Breechclout

Aprons

How to Get Started

When creating his first out-fit, the beginner craftsman is faced with the task of choosing and making components with very little knowledge in his posses-sion. Thus, we have created this section with a focus on fairly detailed instructions for the most basic of outfit components. In general, we have tried to keep the crafts-manship straightforward and have relied upon readily available materials. Beyond that we suggest that the first project be a set of aprons and we have listed the steps needed to eas-ily make the set:

Step 1. Go to a fabric store and purchase:
  (a) 1 yard of dark blue wool;
  (b) 1 package of red ½" double-fold bias tape;
  (c) Spools of red and dark blue cotton or cotton/poly blend thread.

Step 2. Get help from a parent, sibling, or neighbor who has a sewing machine:
  (a) Show your helper the pictures and instructions about aprons (Pages 69 to 71) in this book;
  (b) Ask your helper to use the materials you pur-chased in Step 1 to help you make the aprons;
  (c) Try them on with one of your belts—and smile at your success!

Alternative Step 2. Take the materials purchased in Step 1 along with Xerox copies of the pictures and instructions for aprons from this book to a dry cleaning shop that does sewing/alterations. Ask them if they can make the aprons according to the instructions. It is likely that the charge for doing this will be modest.

Another Alternative Step 2. Learn how to use a sewing machine or do the sewing with a simple needle. This is something that, having learned it, will likely serve you well for many years.

This photograph, taken in 1898, shows a group of Sioux warriors most of whom are wearing the type of leggings described in this chapter. Note also the breechclouts made of selvedge edge wool.

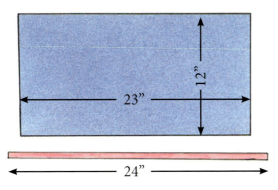

1

Making a Set of Aprons

Materials: Cut out two rectangles of dark blue wool cloth that are each 12" wide by 23" long. Cut four pieces of ½" wide bias tape that are 24" long.

HOW TO:

1. The front and back aprons are exactly the same dimensions. Start with one wool rectangle and two bias tape strips. Iron the bias tape strips flat and pin each strip to a long edge of a wool rectangle.

2. Using a common sewing needle, and thread that is the same color as the bias tape, sew a running stitch the entire length of the wool rectangle. Trim the excess bias tape so that it is even with the end of the wool.

3. Fold over three inches of one of the short edges of the wool rectangle and iron it down so there is a crease at the top of the apron. Make a chalk line 2" from the upper edge of the apron and pin along this line. Using dark blue thread, sew down the folded over edge along the chalk line. This creates the belt loop at the top of the apron.

4. Finish the second apron in the same way.

The aprons are now ready to wear using a regular belt or a wide buckskin lace.

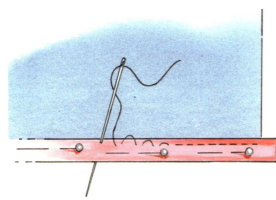

2

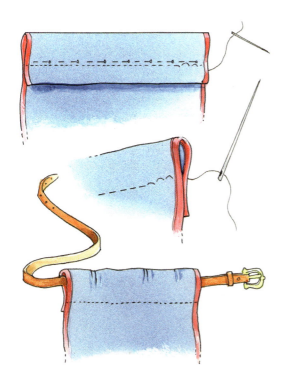

3

4

On this page we show examples of aprons with descriptions of the styles common to each of the three Plains regions outlined in this book.

Central Plains

In this area the front of the apron should be decorated with horizontally placed ribbons of varying widths and colors along with a vertical edging of a single color. Brass sequins and decorative coins can also be added. The example shown here is most typical and uses only ribbons.

Northern Plains/Plateau

In this area the front of the apron should be decorated with horizontally placed ribbons and rickrack of varying widths and colors along with vertical edging of a single color. Brass-colored sequins and decorative coins can also be added. The example here shows all of these features.

Southern Plains

In this area the aprons tended to be long and very plain, featuring only vertical edging of a single color. Note that rainbow selvedge edge tradecloth is only used on the Southern Plains.

Apron that is made with the dimensions described on page 69.

Apron made slightly wider than described on page 69.

Aprons made slightly narrower than described on page 69.

Plain blue wool with ribbon edging.

Fake white selvedge edge made of white ribbon.

Reproduction tradecloth with white selvedge edging.

Horizontal ribbons added.

Brass-colored sequins and coins added.

Quilled panel added.

Apron Progression

On this page we will demonstrate the progression of a front flap of a set of Central Plains aprons from beginning through intermediate to advanced.

A beginning apron is quite simple with just a belt loop and ribbon edging. One version is made from blue wool. A second version is made from blue wool with a fake white selvedge edge applied (This can be made with white wool or white ribbon). The third version is made from reproduction white selvedge edge trade cloth. This is the best base for a set of aprons since intermediate and advanced versions would normally use selvedge edge material. Thus, the progression is best served with reproduction selvedge edge trade cloth.

The intermediate version is made from the reproduction selvedge edge beginning apron. In order to improve on it, the ribbon edging was removed (a very easy task if one has a seam ripper, a $3.00 tool available at all fabric stores). Then the horizontal ribbons were sewn on followed by re-sewing the ribbon edging.

Adding brass sequins to the intermediate version created an advanced version. It was further enhanced by the addition of decorative coins along the bottom edge.

Finally to enhance the advanced apron even more, a quilled panel has been added. This ornamentation is seen in vintage Central Plains photographs, but only rarely.

Making a Set of Leggings - Introduction

Once you have completed a set of aprons, the next item to consider is a pair of leggings. These are as easy to make as aprons and we will describe the process in detail.

Note this vintage photo showing a Sioux warrior wearing an undecorated breechclout and leggings made of selvedge edge tradecloth. Note also the two-feather headdress. This outfit could fit easily into the Central Plains Beginning Outfit section of this book!

Vintage photo showing simple, undecorated breechclout and leggings.

Cutting Leather Lacing

In this photograph we see two uses of the type of lacing described on this page: spiral-wrapping of the bottom of the cuff and the outside-leg closing on a panel legging.

Before you go any further, you should learn how to make leather lacing as you will need this kind of lacing for many projects in this book and other Indiancraft projects.

Materials

You need soft leather such as buckskin for making lacing. The best buckskin is available from mail order supply houses. Commercially tanned hides from deer, elk, antelope, and even buffalo are available. However, soft deerskin/buckskin is an excellent choice for most projects. Brain tanned hides are superior because they are stronger and the most authentic, although they are very expensive. At the other end of the scale are old leather jackets, sometimes found at flea markets: they can be satisfactory if chosen carefully. Note that it is wise to save any scrap hide from projects since these can be perfect for making lacing.

Tools

A pair of heavy-duty sharp scissors can be used, but the best choice is a pair of scissors specially designed for cutting leather. This type of scissors is available from leathercraft stores and mail order trading posts.

How To:

1. Round off the corners of a piece of soft leather.

2. Using scissors cut the edges of the leather piece continuously, judging the width of the lacing you desire by eye. As you get more experience, you will get better at making uniform lacing.

3. The long lace can now be cut into the lengths you need for your project.

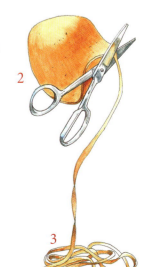

Central and Southern Plains Cloth Leggings

These instructions are for the dark blue wool cloth leggings so commonly found on the Central and Southern Plains. They are easy to make, simply requiring cutting, folding, and sewing a straight-line seam. The measurements given here are suitable for an average teenager. They can be readily adjusted to fit shorter or taller persons.

Central and Southern Plains leggings are most commonly sewn along the seam. However, Northern Plains/Plateau leggings are tied at the seams using buckskin laces. The sides of the flaps and the leg openings are bound with colored cloth tape or ribbon. The binding on the flaps is often a darker color, whilst the binding on the leg openings is often a light color.

If you are using reproduction selvedge edge tradecloth, use the solid white edge for both Central and Southern Plains leggings and rainbow edge for Southern Plains only. The selvedge edge always runs the length of legging and not across the bottom.

Materials

 1 piece of dark blue wool (almost black) 56" x 33"
 4 yards of ½" wide double fold red bias tape
 2 yards of ½" wide double fold light colored bias tape
 1 spool each of thread to match wool and bias tapes

Tools

 Yardstick, tailor's chalk, scissors, steam iron, straight pins, sewing needle or sewing machine.

How To:

1. Cut wool cloth
  2 pieces—24" x 33"
  4 pieces of dark bias tape—2" x 22"
2. Cut bias tape
  2 pieces of light bias tape 26" long
  Red—4 strips, 36"
3. Repeat step 2 with the bias tape at the bottom with the steam iron and sew them on the long edges of the large wool pieces. Cut the ends even with the wool.
4. Remove the creases in the yellow bias tape strips with the steam iron and sew one on the short edge of the wool piece. Cut the ends even with the wool.
5. Sew one of the wool strips (2" x 22") to the top of one of the large wool pieces. Repeat for the second one. These straps fasten the leggings to a belt.
6. Fold the wool pieces so the long edges are together evenly. Iron down the fold.

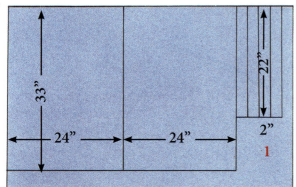

74

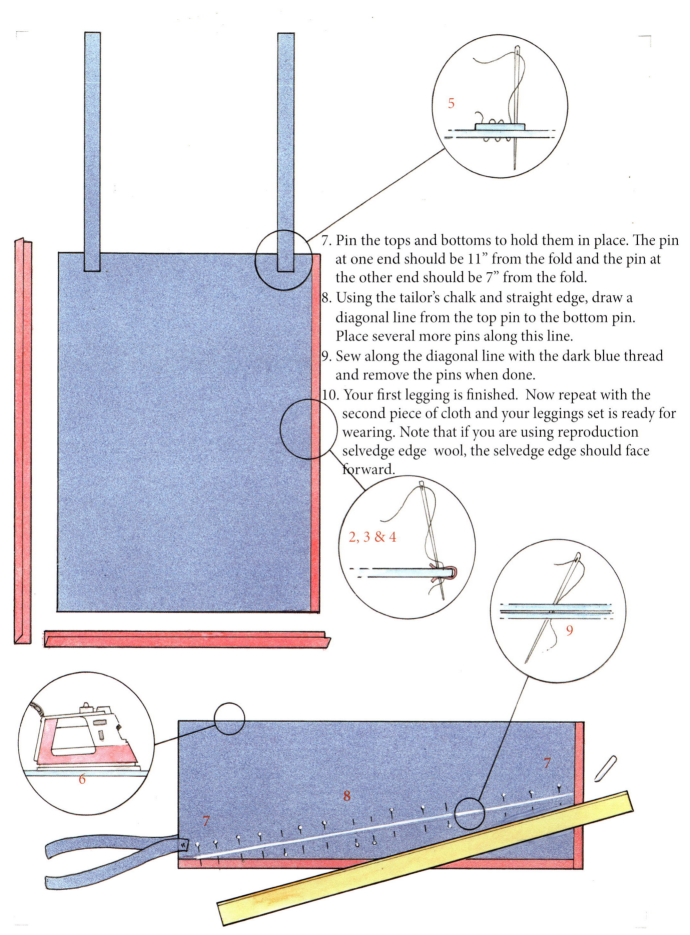

7. Pin the tops and bottoms to hold them in place. The pin at one end should be 11" from the fold and the pin at the other end should be 7" from the fold.

8. Using the tailor's chalk and straight edge, draw a diagonal line from the top pin to the bottom pin. Place several more pins along this line.

9. Sew along the diagonal line with the dark blue thread and remove the pins when done.

10. Your first legging is finished. Now repeat with the second piece of cloth and your leggings set is ready for wearing. Note that if you are using reproduction selvedge edge wool, the selvedge edge should face forward.

5

2, 3 & 4

9

6

7

8

7

Northern Plains/Plateau Panel Leggings

Panel Leggings are unique to the Northern Plains/Plateau areas. The panels on the leggings illustrated here are not decorated. However, you can see several beadwork patterns on the outfits in Chapter 2.

This type of legging is as easy to make as the Central and Southern Plains cloth leggings. For panel leggings, you can begin by cutting the cloth, binding the edges, and folding the leggings using the same technique described for the Central and Southern Plains version on pages 74 and 75. Note, however, that panel leggings have some differences as described below.

Panel leggings differ in the following ways: the dark blue cloth is wider; the edge binding is same color for both the sides and bottoms; the side binding stops about ten inches from the top of the legging; the diagonal seam is made with buckskin ties (instead of sewing with thread); and there is a trapezoidal panel of contrasting color at the bottom of the legging. In the example we show, the legging wool cloth is very dark blue and the trapezoidal panels are red wool.

Materials

> 1 piece of dark blue wool (almost black)—64" x 33"
> 1 piece of red wool—30" x 8"
> 6 ½ yards of ½" dark red double fold bias tape
> 1 piece of buckskin about 8" x 8"—or 6-36" tan cotton shoe laces
> 1 spool each of dark blue thread and dark red thread to match wools
> 1 spool of dark red thread to match bias tape

Tools

> Sharp scissors for cloth, sharp scissors for leather if needed, yardstick, steam iron, tailor's chalk, awl (An ice pick or very sharp nail will also work.), sewing needle or sewing machine

How To:

1. Follow steps 1 through 4 on page 74 (Central and Southern Plains cloth leggings).
2. Cut out a red wool trapezoid that is 15" at the top by 13 ½" at the bottom. The width is 8".
3. Cut 6 yards of 3/16" wide buckskin lacing (See page 73 for instructions). This step is unnecessary if you are using shoe lacing. Cut the lacing in 16 ties (8 for each legging) that are 12" long.

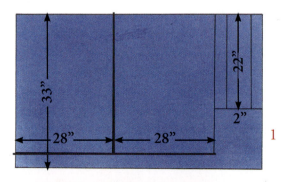

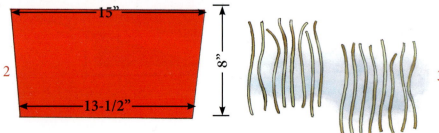

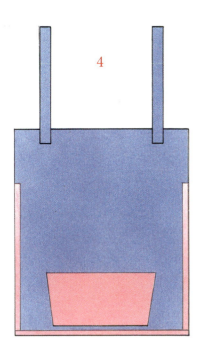

4. Sew the red wool trapezoid near the bottom of the legging. This trapezoid must be centered and placed approximately ½" away from the bottom edge binding.

5. Follow steps 6 though 8 as shown for the Central and Southern Plains Cloth Leggings on pages 74 and 75.

6. At the bottom of the legging use your awl to poke a hole in both layers of wool cloth. This hole should be near a bottom corner of the trapezoid.

7. Poke another hole 3/8" above the first hole. Poke the pointed ends of the laces through the holes and pull them up tight. Keep the ends of the laces even.

8. Tie the laces with a square knot that is close to the wool cloth. Repeat this process, spacing all eight ties 3 ¾" apart. The legging is now closed and ready to wear.

9. When closing the second legging, make sure that you are creating a mirror image. When both leggings are complete, the dangling ends of the laces will be at the back.

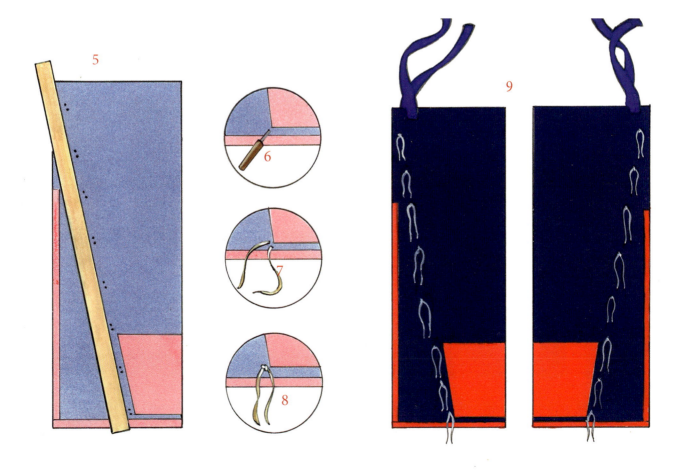

Northern Plains/Plateau Blanket Leggings

Blanket leggings tend to be seen only in the Northern Plains/Plateau areas. The extreme cold weather and the tribes' long association with fur trading establishments such as The Hudson Bay Company made striped blanket leggings a common sight. Broad stripes of varying colors were woven into the blankets, but perhaps the most popular were the white blankets with multi-colored "candy stripes". In fact, on the Northern Plains and Plateau, leggings made from these blankets were probably as popular in their day as jeans are today.

Because these leggings are a project for an intermediate craftsman we have not included detailed instructions for making them. An intermediate craftsman should be able to use the instructions and dimensions for cloth panel leggings for the necessary guidance. On this page we have included an illustration with five possible leggings designs; these are good examples to use when making a pair of leggings. We recommend that you use a medium summer weight blanket for comfort. A second recommendation we will make is to use some ordinary wool for the belt straps: blanket material is too heavy.

Candy stripe leggings (Example 1) were very popular. Stripes or a single band are placed at the bottom of the legging when a panel is not used (Example 2).

Leggings often have a running buckskin lace over the binding, just below the panel (3).

More elaborate blanket leggings feature beadwork (Examples 4 and 5). Thus the panel has a lazy stitched edge and lanes of lazy stitch on the front and back. In this type of legging the colored stripes or bands are positioned at the top of the leggings (Example 5). Another approach is to use floral designs on the front and back of panels. This treatment can be seen on Advanced Outfit One, page 49.

An alternative to beaded edging on panels is ribbon edging. This can be seen on Intermediate Outfit Three, page 44.

The Coup Feather

Few items are as iconic as the golden eagle feather headdresses of the Indians of the Plains. It is an internationally recognized look. Black and white golden eagle tail feathers, placed in various positions in the hair, spoke of battlefield deeds of bravery and of selflessness in the defense of the tribe. These arrays of feathers indicated the status of a warrior in much the same way medals and ribbons worn by modern soldiers do now.

While many types of feathers were worn in the hair by men of all the Plains tribes, the black and white tail feathers of the golden eagle were probably the most revered and certainly what comes to mind. During the 1870-1930 period, one or two golden eagle feathers at the back of the head seems to have been most favored. The feathers were either straight up or at an angle. However, in both vintage photos and vintage ledger drawings one can see other types of feathers, feather combinations, and feather positions that were used.

This unidentified Sioux warrior, wearing a single feather tied in his hair, makes a strong statement.

For the beginning craftsman it is probably easier to make the type of headdress that uses looped feathers simply tied into the hair. Having mastered that, one can advance to the more common upright feather array. This is yet another version of progression.

The vintage photo of Crow King, a Sioux warrior, has been amongst the authors' favorite photos for many years. There is much to study and learn about in this photo. For example, note that the single slightly angled black and white golden eagle feather is elegant in its simplicity. Other items that merit comment are: the long braids (perhaps partially false) wrapped with otter fur; the ring suspended at the bottom of the breastplate, a nice touch; the dentalium shell choker with tacks in the very wide spacers; and the US Military coat with the addition of hair drops at the shoulders. It should be noted here that such a coat, whilst it would be worn at diplomatic occasions, would not be appropriate as part of a dance outfit.

Elegant in its simplicity, a single upright eagle tail feather announces that this man, Crow King, is a warrior.

The second vintage photo on this page shows an unidentified Sioux warrior wearing a golden eagle feather that is pointing down. This effect can be easily copied by using the technique on page 84: making a looped feather and tying the loop directly to the hair at the back or side of the head.

These two vintage photographs give us a rare view of both the front and side of a headdress.

In vintage photos above, we see another Sioux warrior with a two-golden eagle feather headdress. What is remarkable about these photos is that we can see the headdress from two different angles. That allows us to note that at the bases of the eagle feathers are what appear to be owl feathers. They seem to be wrapped around the bases of the eagle feathers. Note that, like Crow King, this warrior also has otter hide-wrapped braids.

The vintage photo below is of a Cheyenne diplomatic delegation to Washington, DC in the 1890s. The three men sitting to the right are clearly each wearing a single horizontal black and white golden eagle tail feather. The feathers have been taken from the outside edges of the eagle's tail. The man at the far left is wearing a feather that is looped and attached so it hangs down.

Single feathers seem to be enough adornment for these diplomats. Note the Southern Plains style buckskin warshirts.

Clusters & Drops

This vintage photograph shows a warrior wearing a cluster consisting of hawk tail feathers with eagle fluffs.

This Central Plains man is wearing a quilled wheel with quilled drops and bead drops.

Cluster and drops are related to coup feather headdresses, but can be made with greater variation. Thus, short feathers from other raptors such as hawks and owls are seen in cluster headdresses such as the one shown in the photo below. Cluster headdresses were found in all three Plains areas, but tend to be found most commonly in the Central Plains. These clusters are usually worn at the back of the head or in groups of two or three feathers at the side of the head as seen on Central Plains Intermediate Outfit Four. This style of cluster requires minimal feather preparation and works very well with feathers of quite different dimensions. The simplest form of these clusters is a grouping of feathers created by attaching loops to the base of the quills. Clusters may be attached directly to loose hair using a leather tie.

Drops can be seen in the hair of the warrior in the photo at the top right. He has one drop made of a quilled wheel with quilled laces and a second drop made of brass beads.

Many kinds of drops are so light they can be attached directly to the hair using thin leather ties. Many of the outfits displayed in this book use drops. Thus, the reader can obtain additional ideas by examining the photos in the Outfits Section.

This photo illustrates how simple it is to make a cluster using looped feathers and a plastic wheel.

A real quilled wheel, imitation eagle fluff, and brass beads make a typical hair drop.

81

Rigs

The dictionary defines a rig as, "Equipment for a special purpose". In this book we will introduce the reader to rigs designed for the special purpose of creating headdresses that are, at once, authentic-looking and easy to make. Beyond that, these rigs provide an excellent alternative to porky roaches whilst maintaining the The Look. For example, note the vintage photo on this page that shows an 1880 Sioux delegation in Washington, DC. Men as important as Little Dog, Red Cloud, American Horse, and Red Shirt are all seen wearing headdresses that can be made using the rigs we describe. Obviously this was a formal occasion, but such headdresses were also regularly used by dancers of this era.

The rigs we have designed can be made from latigo, cowhide, or belting leather. Counterweights are attached to the bottom of the rig to keep the feathers upright or at an angle. Counterweights can be cow tails, buffalo tails, hairpipes, and hair plates. In this book we have provided templates on pages 86 and 87 that will let the craftsman make rigs for a single feather or double feathers. The feathers can be positioned in all of the standard methods used on the Plains. The rig portion of the assembly should be covered with a metal-backed mirror or concho.

Feather headdresses seen in this vintage photo may be emulated by using rigs.

Headbands

Wearing a rig requires the use of a headband. In this era Plains Indians did not use elaborate headbands, but instead they used a plain hide leather lacing. These encircled the head by passing close to the hairline on the forehead and just above the ears, making them less apparent. Note the vintage photos on this page, showing both the front and back of the heads of warriors using headbands.

Headbands securing a rig or hair extension in this period were functional and not designed to be decorative.

This late 19th Century photograph of a Central Plains man shows him wearing a two-feather vertical rig that is held on by a thin leather headband.

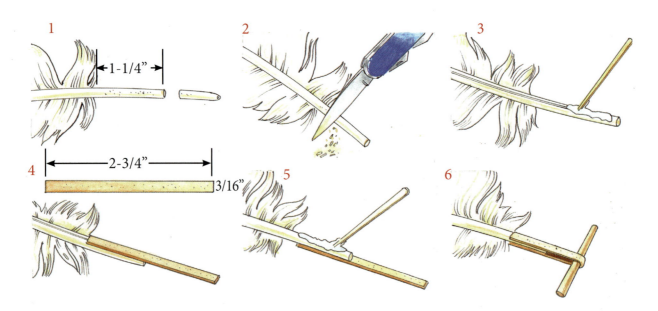

Making a Looped Feather

Perhaps one of the easiest beginning projects is making a loop at the end of a feather. The method shown here not only applies to simple headdresses, but also is a basic step in making a bustle or warbonnet. The traditional method for looping a feather was to use the quill, carved out and bent back upon itself. However, in the old days they were using real eagle feathers, which have a bigger, stronger quill than the turkey feathers used to make imitation eagle feathers. In addition, the eagle feathers were usually freshly removed and, thus, more pliable. The method we show here is much more suited for commercially available imitation eagle feathers.

Materials	Tools	
1 Imitation eagle feather	Scissors	Pocket Knife
Buckskin lacing	Toothpick	3/16" Dowel ca. 3" long
Cream-colored thread	White Glue	Diagonal Pliers

How To:

1. Measure 1 ¼" from the vane of the feather and cut off the excess quill with the diagonal pliers.
2. Using the pocket knife, scrape off the scaly material that clings to the quill. This will provide a rough surface for the glue.
3. Using the toothpick, apply white glue to the quill. Allow the glue to become tacky.
4. Cut a strip of buckskin 3/16" wide by 2 ¾" long. Place the strip onto the glue so that the end of the strip is at the point where the vane begins. Allow to dry thoroughly.
5. Turn the feather over. Apply white glue to the other side of the quill. Allow the glue to become tacky.
6. Place the 3/16" dowel piece at the end of the quill. Bend the buckskin strip over the dowel and on to the glue. Remove the dowel and allow the glue to dry thoroughly.
7. When the glue is thoroughly dry, wrap the buckskin strip in two places with the cream-colored thread. Cut a buckskin lace 1/4" wide by 8" long. Thread the buckskin lace through the hole created by the dowel and tie the feather to your hair.

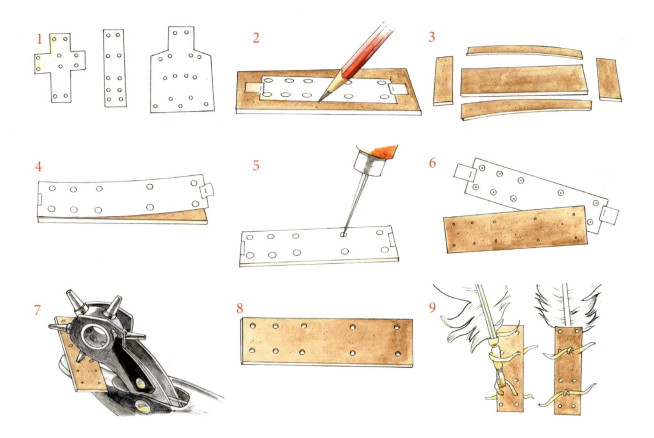

Constructing a Rig and Attaching a Looped Feather

Using a rig allows you to control the placement of coup feathers without having to employ a long, heavy scalp lock. You can wear feathers upright or horizontally and make a headdress featuring multiple feathers. In this book we demonstrate three types of rigs, but once you understand the principle, you can design your own rig pattern to add more feathers and ornaments.

Materials

One old thick belt or some saddle leather
Buckskin lacing to be used for ties

Tools

Masking tape, scissors suitable for cutting leather, fine point pen, hole punch for leather, awl or very sharp nail

How To:

1. Select an actual size pattern from page 86 or 87. We have selected the pattern for a Single Feather Vertical Rig.
2. Copy the pattern at 100% with a copy machine. Using small strips of masking tape, attach the pattern to the leather. Outline the pattern with the fine point pen.
3. Remove the pattern and cut the rig out with the scissors.
4. Re-tape the pattern on the leather cut-out.
5. Using an awl, punch through the center of each circle on the pattern.
6. Remove the pattern. The holes are now marked on the rig.
7. Set the leather punch to the smallest hole and punch out the holes using the awl marks as guides.
8. The rig is now ready for attaching the feather.
9. Cut two buckskin ties 3/16" by 4". Place the feather, underside facing you, onto the rig. Use the second row of holes from the bottom for the tie that goes through the feather loop. Use the second row of holes from the top to secure the feather in the upright position. Finish the ties with square knots. The remaining holes can be used for a headband, concho or circular mirror and counterbalance.

Single Feather Vertical Rig

Assembling the rig is quite simple. This exploded view shows very clearly how to do the assembly. Note that you can use heavy string to tie on the feather, concho, and counterbalance, but the headband must be leather.

The counterbalance in the photo above is made of sisal rope, simulating the long hair from a horse's tail. To make it, simply unravel a length of rope, soak it in hot water to relax the fibers, brush out the wet fibers, and allow them to dry. Next, trim the bottom of the "tail" into a pointed shape. You can dye the sisal red, green, or yellow. You can also make this type of counterbalance from real horsehair, simulated human hair, or real human hair.

Materials

1 Feather	1 Buckskin tie
1 Single Feather	1/4" x 30"
Vertical rig	
4 Buckskin ties	1-3" Concho
3/16" x 4"	1 Counterbalance

How To:

1. Attach the feather to the rig as described on page 85.
2. Make a loop at the top of the counterbalance using the technique described on page 84. Run the 4" tie through the loop.
3. Insert the pointed tie ends into the bottom holes of the rig. Turn the rig over and tie ends with a square knot. The knot should be just tight enough to allow some movement of the counterbalance. This will allow the top of the

counterbalance to be just below the bottom of the rig.

4. Run a 4" tie through the ring in the concho and insert the pointed ends into the holes that are in the third row from the bottom edge of the rig and tie them with a square knot. The concho should be firmly held to the rig.
5. The headband is attached to the rig by inserting the pointed ends of the 30" buckskin lacing through the two holes at the top of the rig.

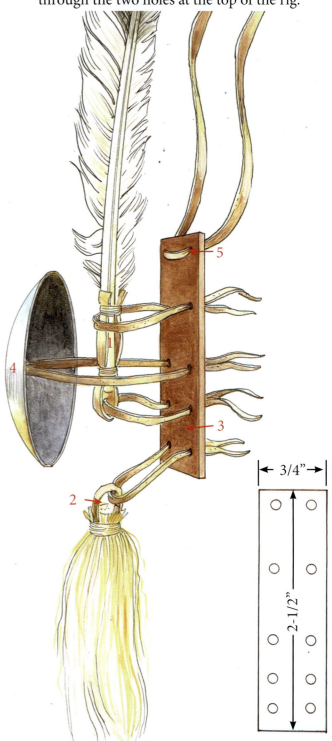

Single Feather Horizontal Rig

The Single Feather Horizontal Rig is just as easy to assemble as the Single Feather Vertical Rig. Note that the cross bar is at a slightly upturned angle. This is because the weight of the feather tends to make it droop downwards.

This counterbalance is made using graduated conchos, purchased from a mail order catalog. The conchos are mounted on a strip of red wool.

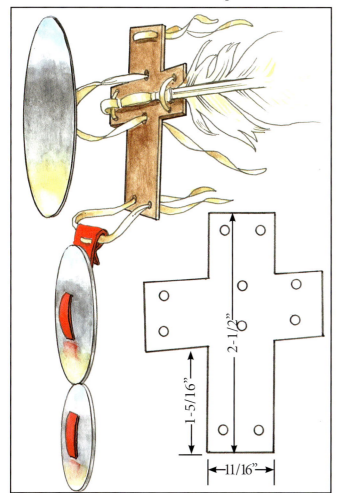

Double Feather Vertical Rig

The Double Feather Vertical Rig looks complicated but it is simply a doubled Single Feather Vertical Rig. Note that the looped feather ends use the same two holes and that the concho ties go through the same two holes as the middle ties on the feathers.

The counterbalance here is just two strands of brass beads and bone hairpipes threaded on buckskin lacing. The rig has a wide bottom base with three holes. The extra holes are there if you choose to use a wide-topped counterbalance such as a buffalo tail or *wapegnaka*.

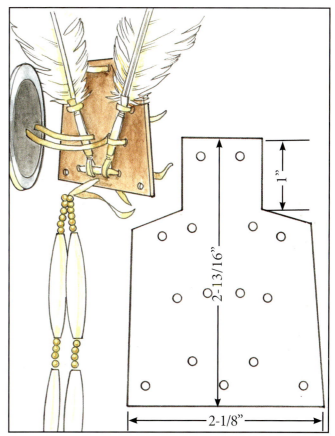

Counterbalances

In the old days the scalp lock served as both a place to secure coup feathers and as a counterbalance to their weight. As haircuts got shorter, another technique was required. The rig is that technique.

In order to complete a rig-type headdress you need a weight at the bottom of the rig to counteract the tendency of the feathers to rotate downward. Some of the outfits in Chapter 2 show coup feathers counterbalanced by long sets of hairplates or by *wapegnakas* that have been beaded or quilled. However, there are simpler approaches and we show some of them here.

This side view of a dancer shows a counterbalance.

A dyed cow tail.

Synthetic human hair.

Strips of rabbit fur.

A real buffalo tail.

Wearing the Roach

Anthropological studies indicate that roaches had their origin along the aboriginal northeast coast of North America. Early explorers and colonists made note of the red-dyed deer tail headdresses worn by tribal warriors and men of importance.

Then, in the early part of the 19th century, such headdresses were seen amongst the Prairie tribes such as the Winnebago, Omaha, and Osage. Prairie roaches of this period were made from horsehair, turkey beards or porcupine guard hair with an outer fringe of deer tail hair. In these early roaches, the deer tail hair was always dyed red.

Amongst some tribes the roach was associated with hunting. The Southern Plains ledger artist, Howling Wolf, depicts men wearing roaches during buffalo and elk hunts. Sometimes the right to wear a roach came with privileges. For example, some roach-wearers were entitled to certain prime cuts of butchered meat.

However, a much more universal significance of the roach was its association with warfare. The Chippewa word for roach means that the wearer is a warrior. Amongst the Osage, certain war party leaders wore roaches. Early Pawnee and Osage ledger art depicts warriors wearing roaches in battle. The Winnebago, Omaha, Osage, and Pawnee required a man to perform certain deeds on the battlefield in order to earn the right to wear a roach. Having earned the right, the warrior would wear his roach to formal occasions such as ceremonies, feasts, and dances.

Thus, the roach was an important symbol and the right to wear it was acquired by prowess, mainly prowess in battle. It was worn by just a few and denoted special status. Its use was spread across the Plains as tribes were given the right to perform the War Dance of the Omaha, Osage, and Ponca. The bustle (a symbol of the battlefield) and the roach (a symbol of the warrior) became the most important components of the War Dance outfit. When the Sioux were given the right to perform the War Dance, the bustle and the roach were included. Interestingly, the Sioux word for roach, *pesa*, means "red top" and refers to the early tradition of dying the deer tail hair red for use on a roach.

Southern Plains ledger art circa 1870-80 shows Kiowa, Comanche, Southern Cheyenne, and Arapaho warriors wearing roaches. By the end of the 19th century, the War Dance had been adopted by nearly all the tribes on the Plains. With this growth in popularity, came the secularization of both the roach and the bustle. They were no longer restricted to those who earned the right to wear them based on battlefield prowess. Also, the deer tail hair used on roaches was no longer exclusively red. Vintage black and white photos show the deer hair with different shades of gray, indicating colors other than red.

A Northern Plains dancer wearing both a roach and a bustle. It is unusual for a Northern dancer to wear his roach so far back, but typically there are no roach feathers. Both dancers are wearing hair extenders attached with thin buckskin headbands.

The roach spreader acts to hold the roach to the head. It also supports the roach feathers.

Roach Spreaders

Roach Spreader is a misnomer: this device is not used to spread the roach. Instead it is used to attach the roach to the wearer's head. Additionally, if there are roach feathers, the spreader will also have sockets attached to accommodate one or two feathers.

Traditionally, roach spreaders were constructed of bone, elk antler, rawhide, German silver, or wood. Substitute materials can be thick belting leather, saddle leather, or sheet metal such as tin cans. Southern Plains roach spreaders can be made of German silver and can be purchased from trading posts.

The sockets for roach feathers are designed to allow the feathers free movement as the wearer dances. Normally they are made from eagle wing bone or other hollow animal/bird bones. They can also be made from spent firearm cartridges. If the spreader is made of German silver, the sockets will also be made of German silver. Substitute materials include metal or plastic pipe of appropriate diameter. A convenient source of hollow bird bones is the Thanksgiving turkey leg bone. Remove any remaining meat from the bone and allow it to thoroughly dry. When the bone is dry, scrape off any remaining meat, cut it to size, remove any marrow that remains, and drill holes as described in the illustrations.

The center and left patterns shown on this page are common shapes for old time rawhide spreaders. The pattern on the far right is not a traditional shape, but we show it for convenience because it can be made from a belt. Select the appropriate pattern and material for your roach and cut it to shape. Drill or punch the holes needed—the number and position will depend on how many roach feathers you plan to use. Each socket will require eight holes, as shown. Attach the socket(s) as shown in the illustrations. Note that the large hole in the front center is used for the tie lace. The two small holes at the back of the spreader are used to attach it to the roach base.

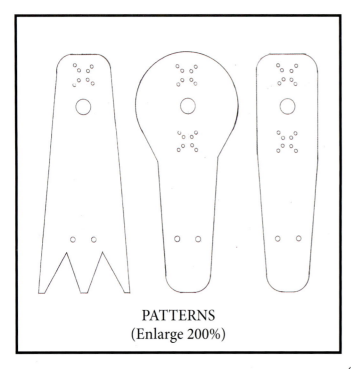

PATTERNS
(Enlarge 200%)

Making a Roach Spreader

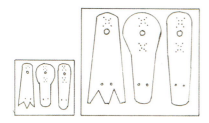

1. On a copy machine, enlarge the patterns by 200%. Cut out the pattern of choice. We chose pattern 3 to be used on a strip of 1-1/2" wide belt.

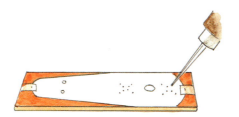

2. Tape the pattern onto the leather. Using an awl, mark the placement of the holes indicated on the pattern.

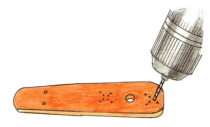

3. Using a drill, make small holes for attaching the tubes with a 1/16" bit. Drill the larger hole shown with a 3/8" bit. And, near the back of the spreader, drill the two holes shown with a 1/8" bit.

4. With all the holes drilled, the spreader base is completed and looks as shown.

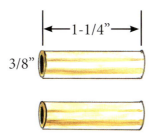

5. To prepare the feather sockets, begin by obtaining some plastic tubing that has an inner diameter of at least 3/8". Obtain enough to make two sections that are 1-1/4" long.

6. In each of the two 1 ¼" tubes, drill four 1/16" holes. The holes should be equidistantly spaced and about 1/4" from the bottom of the tube as shown above.

7. Measure up 1/2" from the bottom of the tube and drill two 1/8" holes opposite each other. They should be above the center of two of the 1/16" holes as shown. The sockets are now completed.

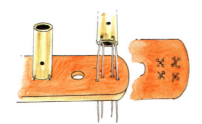

8. Using heavy carpet thread, attach the completed sockets to the spreader as shown. The 1/16" bottom holes should be aligned with their counterparts in the spreader base. Tie square knots as shown.

9. The roach spreader is now complete. To attach the feathers, see page 93. Instructions for attaching the spreader to the roach are on page 94.

Finished roach spreaders. The one on the left is Southern Plains style. It was made from rawhide; a turkey bone was used for the feather socket. The one in the center is commonly found on the Central Plains and Northern Plains/Plateau areas; it was made from an old leather holster and some spent cartridges. The one on the right was made considering materials easily available today. We used an old belt and plastic tubing.

These two roach feathers have had the vanes partially stripped. Colored embroidery thread has been wrapped around the stripped quill.

The two roach feathers in this photo have large fluffs at the base with a combination of rabbit fur strips and small fluffs at the tips.

These two roach feathers feature delicate human hair scalplocks with the ends covered by thin ermine strips.

Roach Feathers

Generally, the black and white (immature) outside tail feathers of the Golden Eagle are considered "roach feathers". One from each side of the tail, one right and one left, is considered a matched pair and was highly prized on the Central Plains. However, it appears that on the Southern Plains the center tail feather is the preferred roach feather. On the Northern Plains, if a roach feather was used, any tail feather was selected. Whilst the immature tail feathers were preferred, mature (dark) feathers were used, too.

The number of roach feathers used varied by area. The Central Plains dancer usually wore two feathers, but sometimes wore only one. The Northern Plains dancer, more often than not, wore none. The Southern Plains dancer usually wore only one feather. Feathers were often undecorated. However, the feathers could be decorated using fluffs, quilled strips, and ermine skin pieces. Sometimes the feathers were partially stripped.

Preparing the Feather Quill

There are many traditional ways of fastening the roach feather to the socket. We have chosen a modified traditional method here due to its ease and the type of feathers that will be used. We must use imitation golden eagle feathers made from turkey feathers. Compared to real eagle feathers, turkey feathers have thinner, weaker quills. We compensate for this weakness by cutting off the tip of the feather quill and inserting and gluing a tightly fitting dowel into the hollow. The dowel is held in by a combination of friction and glue. A hole is drilled through the bottom of the dowel. The feather is attached to the socket as shown in the drawings by using heavy thread. The thread is knotted in a manner that will allow the feather to move freely. Note that it is important to firmly attach the feather to the socket and the socket to the spreader because it is very bad form to have a feather fall to the ground.

Preparing the Feather Quill

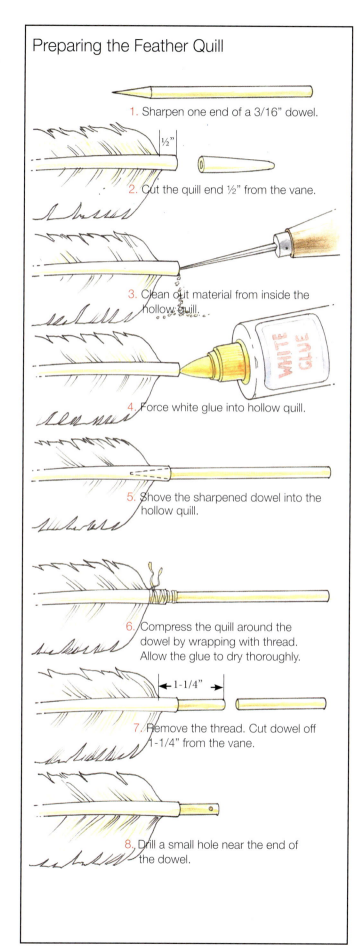

1. Sharpen one end of a 3/16" dowel.

½"

2. Cut the quill end ½" from the vane.

3. Clean out material from inside the hollow quill.

WHITE GLUE

4. Force white glue into hollow quill.

5. Shove the sharpened dowel into the hollow quill.

6. Compress the quill around the dowel by wrapping with thread. Allow the glue to dry thoroughly.

←1-1/4"→

7. Remove the thread. Cut dowel off 1-1/4" from the vane.

8. Drill a small hole near the end of the dowel.

This elk antler spreader and roach feather are good Southern Plains examples. The hole in the bottom of the feather can be clearly seen. The hole in the side of the socket is visible in the assembled roach.

Tying the feather into the Socket

1. Use heavy thread.

2. Tie the knot loosely so the feather will move freely.

93

Attaching the Roach to the Head

There are several ways to attach a roach to one's head. We discuss the most common way here: using ties. When tying on a roach you need to remember an important rule of wearing a roach: the base of the roach does not comform to the back of the head. Instead, it falls in a graceful arc from the top of the head to the end of the roach base.

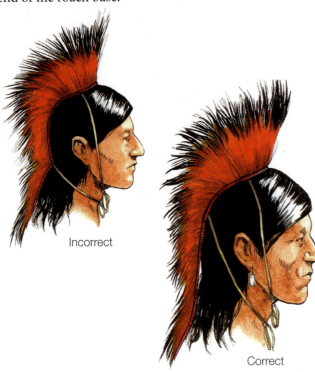

Incorrect

Correct

Preparing the Roach and Spreader for Use

The instructions to the right will allow you to set up your roach and spreader for use. In order to do so, you will also need to insert some ties in your roach and learn how to attach the cheek tie to the spreader and insert it in your roach.

There is a "roach hole" at the center of the roach base near its front. There is a corresponding "spreader hole" near the front of the spreader as well. Both of these holes are used for the cheek tie and serve as common reference points for all measurements.

Most commercial roaches have a base made by sewing strands of cotton rope together. In the following instructions, we describe punching holes in the base. It is convenient to punch such holes between the strands of the rope.

1. The first step is to insert the stabilizer tie. This is done by punching two holes in the roach base 3" from the center of the roach hole. These holes correspond to the two stabilizer holes at the back of the spreader; they are about 1/2" apart.

2. Prepare the stabilizer tie by cutting a lace 3/16" wide by 8" long. Turn the roach so the underside is facing you and insert one end of the tie into one of the stabilizer holes of the roach base; repeat with the other end of the tie and the second stabilizer hole. Pull the ends flush with the roach base.

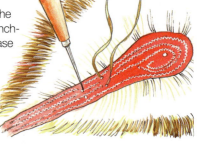

3. The next step is to insert the neck tie. This is done by punching two holes in the roach base about 4" from the center of the roach hole—again, about 1/2" apart.

4. Prepare the neck tie by cutting a lace 3/16" wide and 30" long. This is inserted in their respective holes similarly to the stabilizer tie, but from the top side of the roach base.

5. Prepare the cheek tie by cutting a lace 3/16" wide and 30" long. This lace is inserted in the spreader hole, but it is looped around the front feather socket in order to anchor it. The tie is pulled firmly against the socket, making sure that the ends are even. Then insert the cheek tie ends in the roach hole of the base, making certain that spreader is snug against the base.

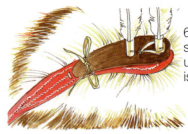

6. The final step is to tie the spreader to the roach base using the stabilizer tie. This is secured with a bow knot.

94

Roach Placement

In general, there were some regional differences in the placement of the roach on a man's head. We have outlined those differences on this page. However, as in all human endeavors, there is variation in custom. Thus, it makes sense to look at many photos of men from a given area before selecting a different placement than suggested here.

Northern Plains/Plateau

On the Northern Plains/Plateau, roaches were about 15 inches at the base and they were usually placed close to the hairline at the forehead. The porcupine guard hair was often quite long and lay nearly flat. Often there were no roach feathers, but one or two roach feathers could be used.

Central Plains

On the Central Plains, the roach was commonly worn in center of the head. The spreader would usually feature two black and white golden eagle tail feathers, which were normally the two outside edge feathers. Less commonly, only one of these feathers was used. The roach was usually modest in length, approximately 10 inches at the base.

Southern Plains

On the Southern Plains, roaches tended to be shorter, 6 inches at the base, and they were worn towards the back of the head. A single center golden eagle tail feather was very common.

95

A WORD FROM THE AUTHORS

For us, the culture and crafts of the Plains Indians has been magnetic. The history, past and present, of these indigenous Americans has been compelling. Their culture is unique to America and should be admired by all. We hope this book will give many people, especially youth, an opportunity to both understand a part of that culture and to emulate it in a manner that is, at once, creative and respectful of these time-honored traditions.

M. S. "Mike" Tucker earned his Bachelor of Arts in History and Anthropology at California State University, Sonoma. His career included 24 years as the Curator of Collections and Exhibits for the California State Indian Museum. His interest in Native American material culture began in the late 1950s when he was a Boy Scout. After serving in the United States Navy, Mike moved to Oklahoma where he was an active participant in powwows and was a co-publisher of American Indian Crafts and Culture Magazine. He is nationally recognized for his excellent pamphlet on Old Time Sioux Dancers.

Joe W. Rosenthal earned his Bachelor of Science Degree in Chemistry from the University of California and his PhD in Chemistry whilst a student at Yale and Harvard Universities. Following postdoctoral studies at UCLA, he began his professional career in the petroleum industry. His interest in Native American material culture began as a Boy Scout in the 1950s. Joe has continued his affiliation with the Boy Scouts as a member of Ut In Selica Lodge and by serving on the American Indian Activities Staff at National Order of the Arrow Conferences.

PHOTO CREDITS

Page 2, National Anthropological Archives; *Page 6,* Charles M. Russell, Authors' Collection; *Page 7,* Amos Bad Heart Bull, University of Nebraska Press and F.A. Rinehart, Authors' Collection; *Page 9,* F.A. Rinehart, Authors' Collection; *Page 12,* E.S. Curtis, Authors' Collection, and Museum of the American Indian, Heye Foundation; *Page 13,* Ronald McCoy, Kiowa Memories Images from Indian Territory, 1880, University of Washington Press and Colin Taylor, The Plains Indians, Bedrick Publishing Company; *Page 14,* C.M. Russell, Authors' Collection; *Page 68,* F.A. Rinehart, Authors' collection; *Page 72,* David F. Barry, State Historical Society of North Dakota; *Page 79,* Photographers Unknown, National Anthropological Archives.; *Page 80,* Photographers Unknown, National Anthropological Archives.; *Page 81,* Gertrude Kaesebier, National Anthropological Archives.; *Page 82,* Photographer Unknown, National Anthropological Archives.; *Page 83,* John A. Anderson, University of Oklahoma Press; *Page 89,* Milwaukee Public Museum; *Page 95,* O'Neill Photo Company, Authors' Collection and F.A. Rinehart, Authors' Collection; Joseph K. Dixon, The Wanamaker Collection.